Coex120

MGB

MGB

A Comprehensive Owner's Manual

STUART TURNER
AND
JOHN ORGAN

LONDON
G. T. FOULIS & CO. LTD
1-5 PORTPOOL LANE EC1

First published April 1968

©

STUART TURNER
AND JOHN ORGAN
1968

SBN 85429 075 3

Printed in Great Britain by The Anchor Press Ltd.,
and bound by William Brendon & Son Ltd.,
both of Tiptree, Essex

CONTENTS

ILLUSTRATIONS

ACKNOWLEDGEMENTS

The Authors are indebted to many people who share their enthusiasm for the MGB and have helped in various ways with the preparation of this book, but particular mention must be made of the following:

Former colleagues at the MG Car Company, Roy Brocklehurst, Neville Challis, Den Green, Nobby Hall, Norman Higgins, Cliff Humphries, Barry Jackson, Terry Mitchell, Bob Staniland, Basil Wales, Doug Watts and Tommy Wellman. Secretary Wilson McComb of the MG Car Club and Editor Stuart Seager of *Safety Fast*.

Thanks, too, to Allen Campbell of Ferodo, John Smith of Lucas, Bob Burdon of British Motor Holdings (U.S.A.) Inc. of New Jersey, Peter Millard of British Motor Holdings Canada Ltd, Toronto, as well as to David Marshall and Alec Poole. To BMC Photographic Department for help with the plates, to the Nuffield Press for permission to reproduce most of the line drawings, and finally to Diana Organ for typing the manuscript.

CHAPTER 1

POST-WAR PROGRESS

The MG car factory, a division of the British Motor Corporation (now the British Leyland Motor Corporation), was created by Lord Nuffield as an offshoot of his original Morris Garage (Oxford). Starting life officially in 1930, and retaining the letters MG, the factory quickly became renowned for the characteristic body shape and radiator styling of its cars.

To the MG company the 1930s were golden years of achievement, for not only were many races won with factory-entered cars but numerous international speed records were also taken. By the time World War II curtailed production of the then current TB model, the marque had become well established and nearly 30 different models had been produced.

When, in the era of post-war shortages and austerity, Abingdon resumed production with a sports model (the TC) as the factory's only product, success seemed by no means certain. The TC, however, became a big favourite in America and, with the dollars it earned, helped Britain as well as the MG company.

1947 saw the $1\frac{1}{4}$ litre four-seater Y-type saloon introduced. With rack-and-pinion steering and independent front suspension, it set a new standard for small family saloons and when production ceased in 1953 approximately 8700 had been built.

The immediate post-war car, the TC model, was duly improved by incorporating some of the Y-type features, and became the TD; like its forerunner, it was a good export model to North America.

During the early post-war period many MGs were seen regularly at race tracks and hill climbs in Britain and America, but they were all privately owned, for the factory was unable to give any support beyond advice and encouragement. In 1950 George Phillips, a keen and experienced competitor in races and hill climbs, drove his rebodied TC at Le Mans to finish 18th in general classification and second in class. Although a fine performance, Phillips was convinced that it could be bettered. Abingdon therefore agreed to build him a car for the 1951 event and Sidney Enever, MG top designer, set to work and designed a new streamlined body which was duly fitted to a TD chassis. The car, registration number UMG 400, was powered by a highly-tuned Morris XPAG engine. The body was fitted with aero screens and the car was a fine-looking model, though a great departure from the traditional MG style.

To improve upon Phillips' previous performance UMG 400 had to be driven very hard. It did not finish the race, retiring with valve trouble after three hours. In spite of the disappointing result the car did some good lap times and was basically sound.

Of necessity design teams have to be far-thinking, for at least 12 to 18 months must elapse from the drawing-board stage of a car to its readiness for production. For some time Sidney Enever had envisaged the end of TD production and, encouraged by the Phillips car, work was started on another model, and project EX 182 came into being with the object of designing a model to replace the TD.

The shape of the new car was based on Enever's newly-designed body which was adapted to fit a new, wider chassis frame. Eventually project EX 182 led to the prototype car (HMO 6) early in 1952. Unfortunately, although the prototype continued to be tested, the project had to be shelved, for the Austin and Morris merger which had taken place in July 1951 resulted in the T range being continued with a restyled and improved model for the 1953 London Motor Show. The car was the TF and, although often regarded as something of a stop-gap model, it incorporated some excellent features and remained in production until 1955.

Meanwhile, due to the merger, and a process of rationalization in the new group, the XPAG engine was discontinued, and the Austin 'B' series engine which had already been adopted for the new (MG) Magnette was therefore fitted to HMO 6.

When the time came to discontinue the TF, Sidney Enever was ready and in July 1954 Project EX 182 went ahead once more to become the MGA.

With a new interest in competition work the British Motor Corporation formed an official Competitions Department at Abingdon and two new cars averaged around 85 mile/h in the Prototype Class in the 24 hour race at Le Mans in June 1955, the car being eventually announced to the public at the London Motor Show in October of that year.

Although a departure from the traditional MG sports-car shape, the MGA retained a separate chassis and body and the car remained in production until 1962; over 100,000 were made during the seven years of production.

New cars and new problems

With any car, fashion alone often dictates a change in design and when the MGA was discontinued and a new model was required, modern production methods demanded a good aerodynamic shape of contemporary style with a unit chassis/body construction.

The Abingdon design team, under Sidney Enever, set to work to draw up the MGB.

After extensive wind-tunnel tests with models, the team produced a well-styled car, lighter in weight than the MGA, but as it had a slightly higher drag coefficient, a more powerful engine was needed to better the performance of its predecessor. The MGB was first available to the public at the London Motor Show in 1962; the GT was introduced in 1965.

Development of the 'B' series engine

The engine of the MGA was based on the Austin Motor Company's successful design for the early post-war A40 Devon and when first used in the MG range of sports cars had a capacity of 1498 cc. It was subsequently developed and the capacity increased first to 1588 cc (with 79 bhp at 5600 rev/min) and then, for the Mark II, to 1622 cc by increasing the bore to 3 in. to give 85 bhp at 5500 rev/min.

For the MGB a new cylinder block was produced, within the original design concept, but permitting a bore size of 3·16 in. to give a capacity of 1798 cc (this was the 18G engine). Further development of the engine incorporated a five main-bearing crankshaft (the 18GB engine) and, to ensure complete reliability, an oil cooler was fitted as standard equipment.

Despite its high performance, the five main-bearing engine is now the smoothest of all the 'B' series engines and is a robust unit capable of producing more power with moderate tuning techniques for a marginal decrease in reliability.

When the series IV* MGB was introduced, towards the end of 1967, power units designated 18GD and 18GF were fitted. Although basically the same as the 18GB range of engines, the rear-engine bearer plate is different, to accommodate a new later-type gearbox (see page 12), but all other parts in the GD range remain the same as the 18GB engines and are interchangeable.

The 18GF engine, however, is also fitted with an exhaust-emission control to meet the requirement of the American clean-air act. The system consists of injecting air into the exhaust ports and under some conditions into the inlet manifold to ensure that unburned hydrocarbons are not emitted from the exhaust. Engine dimensions are the same as the 18GB and the 18GD type, but extra

---

* Series IV cars have car-number prefixes: GHN4 (two-seater) GHD4 (GT). The MGA Mark I and II were the first of the series. The MGB until the end of 1967 was designated as series III.

equipment, in the form of an air pump, check valve and gulp valve, is fitted and the cylinder head is modified to take the air injectors. The carburetters are also slightly different, for they incorporate a valve on each throttle butterfly and a restrictor on each mixture-adjusting nut.

Much care and thought has also been put into the development of special safety equipment to ensure that the MGB shall retain its envied position in the North American export market.

CHAPTER 2

A BRIEF TECHNICAL SUMMARY

As with the forerunners of the B.M.C. 'B' series engine, the crankcase and cylinder block of the MGB version is a one-piece casting, the cylinders forming an integral part of the cylinder block.

The cylinder head is detachable with vertically set in-line valves, Siamesed inlet ports and centre exhaust porting. The inlet porting is of the venturi type, reflecting designer Harry Weslake's approach to efficient breathing and combustion.

The cylinder-head combustion chambers are heart-shaped, similar to those of the B.M.C. 'A'-type engine as well as to the earlier 'B' series engines. The prominent squish point between the inlet and exhaust valve (another Weslake innovation) induces a form of deflectionary swirl, whilst the spark plug, set almost diametrically opposite to the squish point but with slight bias towards the inlet valve, ensures that the turbulent charge comes into effective contact with the spark for the most efficient flame propagation.

Two compression ratios are available on the MGB and, whilst the standard engine has a c/r of 8·8:1, an engine is available with different pistons to give a lower ratio (8·0:1). The octane requirement of the car when fitted with the lower c/r engine is 93 while the requirement when the normal c/r engine is fitted is 97–98. (The 'octane' requirement of a car is the lowest octane-value fuel which does not produce detonation at the standard ignition setting, and can be obtained by accelerating in top gear, foot hard down, from 10 mile/h.)

For the tourer fitted with an 8·8:1 c/r engine nothing lower than super-grade fuel (in the U.K. four-star B.S.I. rating 97 octane +) should ever be used. In fact with an engine that is approaching the stage where decarbonization is necessary super-grade plus (five-star rating 100 octane +) should be used, for the octane requirement increases as carbon deposits form in the combustion chamber.

The lower compression-ratio-engined MGB is intended for areas where super-grade fuels are not available. The engine produces about 4 b h p less than the standard engine at 5100 rev/min and a maximum torque of 105 lb ft at 3000 rev/min.

The valves operate in the usual way of B.M.C. pushrod engines through the rocker gear, pushrods and cam followers, from a three-

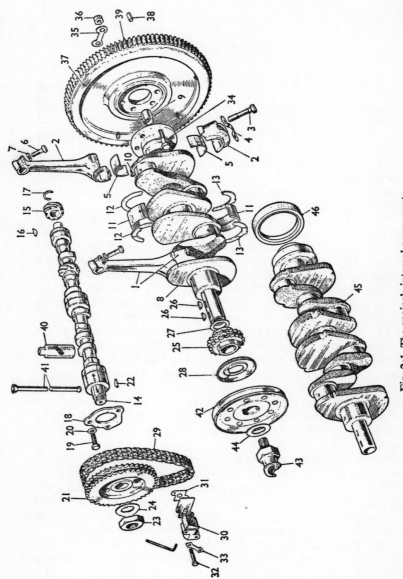

Fig. 2:1. The engine's internal components

KEY TO THE ENGINE'S INTERNAL COMPONENTS

No.	Description
1.	Connecting rod and cap—nos. 1 and 3 cylinders.
2.	Connecting rod and cap—nos. 2 and 4 cylinders.
3.	Screw—cap.
4.	Washer—lock—screw.
5.	Bearing—connecting rod—standard.
6.	Screw—connecting rod clamping
7.	Washer—spring—screw. } (18G/18GA).
8.	Crankshaft.
9.	Bush—first-motion shaft.
10.	Plug.
11.	Bearing—main—standard.
12.	Washer—thrust—upper.
13.	Washer—thrust—lower.
14.	Camshaft.

No.	Description
15.	Gear—tachometer driving.
16.	Key—tachometer gear.
17.	Ring—spring—tachometer gear.
18.	Plate—camshaft locating.
19.	Screw—locating plate to crankcase.
20.	Washer—lock—screw.
21.	Gear—camshaft.
22.	Key—camshaft gear.
23.	Nut—camshaft gear.
24.	Washer—lock-nut.
25.	Gear—crankshaft.
26.	Key—crankshaft gear and pulley.
27.	Washer—packing—crankshaft gear.
28.	Thrower—oil—front—crankshaft.
29.	Chain—timing.
30.	Tensioner—chain.

No.	Description
31.	Joint washer—tensioner.
32.	Screw—tensioner to crankcase.
33.	Washer—lock—screw.
34.	Bolt—flywheel to crankshaft.
35.	Washer—lock—bolt
36.	Nut—bolt.
37.	Flywheel.
38.	Dowel—clutch to flywheel.
39.	Ring gear—starting.
40.	Tappet.
41.	Push-rod.
42.	Pulley—crankshaft.
43.	Nut—pulley.
44.	Washer—lock—starting nut.
45.	Crankshaft } (18GB).
46.	Oil seal

The tachometer gear is not now fitted. All late cars have an electrical impulse type rev counter.

bearing camshaft which is positioned on the left-hand side of the engine.

The camshaft (see fig. 2:1) is driven from the front end by a duplex roller chain which is automatically adjusted, to avoid chain rattle, by means of a Reynolds chain tensioner. This is in the form of a spring-operated rubber slipper which is hydraulically assisted.

End float of the camshaft is controlled by a locating plate set between the front camshaft bearing and the chain wheel.

The valve clearance of ·015 in. is obtained by means of adjusting screws on the rocker arms, excess oil penetration of the combustion chamber, via the valve guides, being prevented by means of oil-sealing rings at the top of the valve stem. The standard camshaft produces a valve timing with an exhaust overlap of 37°, the same as with the 1622 cc forerunner of the 1800 cc engine, but valve lift is slightly increased to ·3645 in. with the same cam-lift of ·250 in.

The barrel-type cam followers fit directly into the cylinder-block casting and are activated by $\frac{1}{2}$ in. wide sine-wave-type cams. Helical gears, on the camshaft, drive the oil pump and distributor, each component having an individual shaft.

Although the 3·5 in. stroke of the 1800 cc engine is the same as its predecessors, the extra capacity is obtained by going to a bore size of 3·16 in. to produce a capacity of 449·5 cubic centimetres per cylinder.

The crankpin diameter of the early three-main-bearing 18G/18GA engine is the same as the 1622 cc 'B' series, but on the 18GB and later series engines the crankpin length is reduced, although the diameter remains the same.

The connecting rods are of the diagonally-split type, which allow the rods to be withdrawn through the cylinder bores. They are offset away from each other in pairs 1–2 and 3–4 to accommodate adequate main bearings in the compact overall length of the crankshaft.

With 18G/18GA engines, clamp-type little-ends are used but, on 18GB, 18GD and 18GF engines, the gudgeon pins are fully floating and are retained in the piston by circlips, the connecting rods being bushed at the little-end.

The lubrication system

Lubrication is by means of pressure from a vertically-mounted eccentric-rotor-type pump, bolted in the left-hand side of the crankcase, the oil being drawn into the pump through an oil strainer submerged in the oil contained in the pressed-steel sump. The oil is delivered through internal oilways to what is normally a non-adjustable relief valve which is secured by a domed hexagon nut on the left-hand side at the rear of the engine. The valve automatically deals with excessive pressure when the engine is cold. The system is designed to supply, under normal operating conditions, not lower than 50 lb/in^2 at moderate road speeds during the life of the engine but a slightly higher pressure is obtained during the initial running period.

Variations in pressure due to climatic conditions are compensated for by the use of the recommended oil grades (see page 164).

From the relief valve, oil passes to the main gallery, of which the filter head is an integral part. The filter is of an adequate free-flow type, sufficient oil for cooling the bearing surfaces and lubrication being ensured at all times, but the filter element should nevertheless be changed at least every 12,000 miles. Under normal conditions, if the element becomes blocked, a relief valve lifts to enable the oil to by-pass the filter.

The supply of oil to the main bearings is obtained from the main oil gallery and goes from there via crankshaft drillings to the big-ends.

The camshaft is also lubricated from the main bearings, while oil to the valve-rocker assembly is fed through drillings in the block and cylinder head, passing through a drilling in the rear rocker-shaft bracket to the hollow rocker shaft, subsequently returning to the sump via the pushrod channels.

The timing sprockets and chain are lubricated by two grooves in the camshaft journal which register with a hole in the camshaft thrust-plate; this allows oil to pass into the timing case twice with each revolution of the camshaft. Surplus oil in the timing case is avoided by a drain which allows excess oil to return to the sump.

The cooling system is pressurized at 7 lb/in^2, the pressure being controlled by a relief valve in the radiator cap. The system functions in the normal way, the water circulating from the bottom of the radiator, passing around the cylinder block and head, to reach the radiator header tank via the thermostat and top water hose. Circulating velocity is assisted by the impellor-type centrifugal pump, situated at the front of the cylinder block and belt-driven from the crankshaft pulley. The passage of air through the radiator is assisted by a fan attached to the water-pump drive pulley.

The operating temperature is maintained within the necessary limits by means of a detachable thermostat fitted in the water outlet at the front of the cylinder head. The opening temperature, which is marked on the body of the thermostat, is set by the manufacturer. The opening temperature cannot be adjusted and if a quicker engine warm-up is required, a thermostat with a higher opening temperature must be fitted.

B

The ignition system

The ignition system is of the usual coil-and-distributor type, the HT current being furnished by a Lucas fluid-filled HA 12 coil mounted on the right-hand front engine-bearer bracket. Distribution of the HT current is by a Lucas one-shank distributor which is fitted with an automatic ignition-timing control.

Carburetters

The carburetters are of the SU HS4 $1\frac{1}{2}$ in. single jet, automatically-expanding-choke type, the size of the main air passage, or choke, over the jet orifice being variable and governed by the amount of throttle opening used against the prevailing load. The size of the jet orifice is controlled by a tapered fuel-metering needle, the profile of which can be varied to suit the requirements of all climates and fuels. The system gives excellent atomization and good consumption figures but, as with all carburetters, it does require servicing, for gum deposits, etc., are just as detrimental to its operation as to multi-jet types of carburetter.

Air filtering for carburation purposes is by means of a dry-paper element incorporated in a large pressed-steel body attached to each carburetter. The inlet manifold is of the usual B.M.C. 'B' series, alloy type, and the exhaust manifolding of the familiar cast-iron form.

Crankcase emission

Fumes from the crankcase are controlled by a breather system consisting of a diaphragm valve connected between the inlet manifold and engine crankcase (see fig. 2:2).

The diaphragm valve system was first fitted to the three-main-bearing (18G) engines, which then became the 18GA range.

With the new system, fresh air enters the engine through a filter in the rocker-cover filler-cap and reaches the crankcase through the pushrod drillings. Fumes, extracted from the engine by manifold depression, pass through an oil separator which prevents oil droplets and oil mist being extracted with the crankcase vapours. A diaphragm control-valve varies the opening to the manifold according to the depression, or pressure existing in the crankcase. When a decrease in crankcase depression occurs, or if pressure exists, the diaphragm valve opens and allows the vapours to be drawn into the inlet manifold. During low engine speeds and high crankcase depression the diaphragm valve closes and restricts the flow of fumes into the inlet manifold.

Exhaust-emission control (GF engines)

The 18GF engine incorporates an exhaust-emission control in the form of exhaust-port air injection (see fig. 2:3).

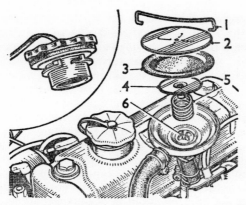

Fig. 2:2. Closed-circuit breathing arrangement. (Inset) Oil filler cap
with combined air filter and the breather control valve

1. Spring clip	4. Metering lever
2. Cover	5. Spring
3. Diaphragm	6. Cruciform guides

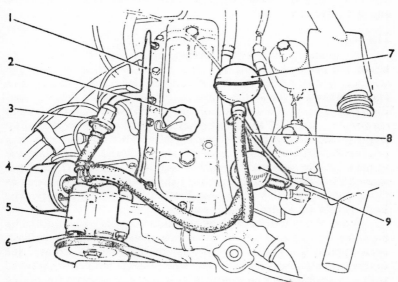

Fig. 2:3. The engine emission control system layout as fitted to 18GF engines.

1. Air manifold	5. Air pump
2. Filtered oil filler cap	6. Relief valve
3. Check valve	7. Crank-case emission valve
4. Emission air cleaner	8. Vacuum sensing tube
9. Gulp valve	

Air is pressure-fed from a belt-driven rotary-vane air pump situated at the front top right-hand side of the engine. The air enters the pump through a dry-type element filter. Should the pump produce excess pressure a relief valve discharges the excess to the atmosphere. From the pump the air passes via a check valve (which protects the pump from any back flow of exhaust gases) to the injector manifold and thence to the exhaust port of each cylinder.

Air is also injected into the inlet manifold under certain conditions and a branch line from the air pump runs to a gulp valve and then to the inlet manifold. When the throttle is closed and manifold depression is suddenly increased, hydrocarbons in the exhaust emission would normally be high, but the gulp valve opens briefly and air is injected into the manifold to ensure that the mixture remaining in the inlet manifold is adequately burned on entry to the combustion chamber. The gulp valve is controlled by a vacuum-sensing pipe which maintains a depression directly to the underside of the gulp-valve diaphragm and through a bleed hole to the upper side. A sudden increase in depression opens the valve, but the bleed hole quickly allows the difference in depression to equalize and the valve closes again.

The body

Of all-steel unitary construction, apart from the bonnet, or hood, the body of the MGB is made from pressings of 20-gauge steel on British-made, American-designed Hamilton, Toledo and Danby presses at the British Motor Holdings Group's Pressed Steel Fisher Company's factory at Swindon in Wiltshire. On the GHN4 (two-seater) and GHD4 (GT) bodies the gearbox tunnel is slightly larger to accommodate the rather bigger gearbox (which came into production with the 18GF and GD engines) and to facilitate the fitment of the automatic gearbox (optional). The GT body is assembled at Swindon, but panels for the tourer version are taken to Coventry for assembly at another Pressed Steel Fisher factory. The body panels are joined by spot welding.

When the bodies have been assembled they are rustproofed by an immersion process and after various protective undercoats have been applied the bodies are sprayed to the requisite colour, the tourer with an air-drying cellulose, while the GT bodies are sprayed with a synthetic paint and have to pass through an oven for drying and hardening.

Body components

The facia panel is detachable, although its removal necessitates dismantling the heater controls, the speedo cable and the wiring harness. However, access to the dashboard instruments, for such things as panel-bulb replacement, merely entails reaching behind the driver's side of the facia panel.

Late cars are fitted with bi-metal instrumentation for the fuel and temperature gauges, but these instruments are not interchangeable with the old type. The instrumentation consists of a voltage stabilizer to which are connected individual transmitter units that operate the separate fuel and temperature indicators. The instruments on cars fitted with this type bear the coding BF for bi-metal fuel and BT for bi-metal temperature.

The heater, which is an optional extra, is mounted on the bulkhead platform. Fresh air is supplied from the front scuttle intake to the heater air box, via body ducting, and after passing through the heater radiator matrix it goes to the windscreen demist tubes via ducting tubes, and to the interior of the car through body ducting and outlet flaps. The amount of air to both the windscreen and the car is governed by a rotary control on the dashboard which operates a flap in the heater box. Hot water to supply the heater radiator is obtained from the engine cooling system and another control on the dashboard operates a valve which varies the flow of hot water so that the temperature can be controlled.

The electrical system

Although on cars with the chassis number prefix of GHN4 or GHD4 the electrical system is of the 12 volt negative earth type, the system on previous cars is of the positive earth return type, in either case the current being carried in one direction by the body of the vehicle except where insulated components require the use of wiring. Two 6 volt batteries are provided which are wired in series and are carried beneath the flooring at the rear of the seats. An access panel for servicing, or removing, the batteries is held in position by quick-release fasteners.

The electrical wiring is by a Lucas harness, made up according to the standard Lucas colour scheme. Feed wires, of which there are nine, consist of one colour only, whereas the colours from switches have a coloured tracer (see wiring diagram). Return or earth leads are black.

The dynamo (or alternator on Series IV cars) is belt-driven from the crankshaft pulley, belt-tension adjustment being obtained by means of a slotted link connecting the dynamo (or alternator) front plate to the engine bearer plate. Voltage control on cars fitted with a dynamo is by an RB 340-type Lucas current/voltage regulator mounted on a bracket secured to the right-hand wing valance.

Operation of the starter, which is mounted on the rear engine plate and engages the flywheel by means of a sliding pinion device, is obtained through a second position on the ignition switch. The system works through a solenoid fitted to the right-hand wing valance.

The steering gear

The steering is by direct-acting rack and pinion, mounted on the front-suspension cross-member, and consists of a cross-shaft mounted in a housing which is operated by a toothed pinion to which the inner steering column is attached by a universal coupling. Adjustment for wear is not necessary and, apart from very early cars, periodic lubrication is not required.

On GHN4 cars and GHD4 cars, fitted with the 18GF engines, the steering column is of the latest safety type with an expanded-metal mesh centre designed to collapse smoothy under predetermined load.

Gearbox and clutch

The four-speed manually-operated gearbox which is fitted to cars with a chassis number prefix of GHN3 or GHD3 has synchro-mesh on top, third and second gears. The gearbox is bolted at the front end to the rear engine-mounting plate and is supported at the rear by two rubber mountings that locate on brackets attached to the de-tachable cross-member. The alloy clutch housing, which contains the 8 in. diaphragm clutch, is cast integrally with the gearbox.

The clutch is a Borg & Beck single-driven plate type, incorporating the normal pressure-plate and diaphragm-spring cover assembly and although the clutch is basically the same on all late models, the gearbox on late cars with a GHN4 or GHD4 chassis number prefix is equipped with syncromesh on first gear.

The clutch driven plate consists of a splined hub connected to a flexible steel plate through torque-reaction damper springs assembled around the hub to help absorb power shocks and torsional vibration. The friction facing material is riveted to the plate in the usual manner.

The diaphragm spring is held between two annular rings which provide the fulcrum points when the clutch is operated.

The overdrive

The Laycock de Normanville overdrive (an optional extra) is controlled electrically through a toggle switch. Basically the unit comprises a hydraulically-controlled epicyclic gear train housed in a casing attached to the rear of the gearbox. It shares a common oil supply with the gearbox and does not require filling separately.

The gearbox (or overdrive if fitted) output flange connects directly to the propeller shaft by four bolts and nuts.

The propeller shaft

The propeller shaft is of the Hardy Spicer type with a universal joint at each end. The front end of the shaft, which connects to the gearbox output flange and holds the front universal, is splined and removable from the main shaft.

Each universal joint consists of four needle-roller assemblies running in a four-arm spider, each arm comprising a bearing journal. Fig. 2:4 depicts the sealed type, which do not require greasing. On early cars a nipple, which should be greased during the normal servicing period, is fitted to the yoke.

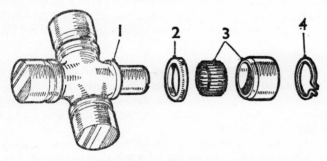

Fig. 2:4. A universal joint bearing—sealed type

1. Journal spider   3. Needle rollers and bearing
2. Rubber seal   4. Circlip

The rear axle

The rear axle on the two-seater (prior to chassis number 129287, wire wheels, and chassis number 132463, disc wheels) is of the three-quarter floating type incorporating a hypoid final drive. The axle casing is attached to the rear spring by 'U' bolts and is rubber-mounted. On GT cars and tourers with later chassis numbers than those quoted, although the axle is mounted in the same manner, the axle is of the tubed semi-floating type, the crown wheel and pinion being completely different from the earlier axle; the parts are not interchangeable.

On tourers prior to July 1967 the differential bearings and pinion bearings are pre-loaded and adjustable by shims. The pinion position in relation to the crown wheel is by spacing washer, the backlash being adjustable by shims. On all late cars adjustment of the rear-axle bearings, and the position of the pinion in relation to the crown wheel, is by means of spacing washers which are available in various thicknesses.

Wheels and wheel bearings

The MGB may be ordered with disc wheels or wire wheels, but the wheels are not interchangeable. With disc wheels, taper roller bearings support the front hubs; four studs pressed into each hub hold the road wheel in place. The brake disc is secured to the hub by nuts and bolts.

The wheel bearings are adjustable by means of shims, interposed in conjunction with a spacer, between the outer and inner bearings. The hubs are fitted at the inner end with oil seals.

The wire-wheel hubs have the same method of wheel-bearing adjustment, but the outer end of the hub takes the form of splines and a coarse thread which holds the wheel-retaining caps, the right-hand side having a left-hand thread and the left-hand side a right-hand thread.

The rear suspension

The rear suspension is by semi-elliptic leaf springs, the front of each spring being bolted through a Silent-bloc bush to a spring hanger attached to the body, while the rear end of each spring is attached to the body by a shackle assembly which is fitted with flexing-type rubber bushes.

The springs are attached to the axles by 'U' bolts, each spring being rubber-mounted and located by a flanged mounting rubber and the spring centre bolt.

Spring shock is dampened by the rear shock absorbers which are fitted to the body side-members. Each shock absorber is attached to the rear axle by a connecting arm which fits on to a plate held in position at the base of the rear spring by the two 'U' bolts which also retain the rear springs.

The front suspension

Most owners will be acquainted with the type of independent front suspension, which is of the wishbone-and-coil-spring type, similar to that of the old MGA, but, as the 'B' is of mono-construction, the suspension units are mounted one on each end of a rubber-mounted cross-member (see fig. 2:5) instead of to a member which is integral with the chassis.

Each suspension unit is assisted by a double-acting hydraulic damper. The lower end of the coil spring is retained by a pan fitted between the lower wishbone arms; at the top, the spring is located by a spigot bolted to the underside of the cross-member.

The wishbone arms are rubber-mounted at the inboard end

and are retained on a pivot bolted to the cross-member, while the
outer ends of the arms are bolted, through a bearing assembly, to
the lower end of the swivel pin.

The top of the swivel pin is secured to the outer arms of the
damper through a fulcrum pin and rubber bushes. The latter are

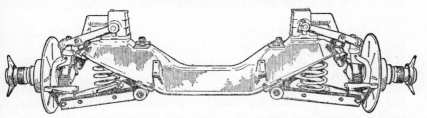

Fig. 2:5. The front suspension cross-member and the suspension units

contained in an upper trunnion link which is secured to the swivel
pin by a hexagon nut.

The front- and rear-suspension method on the GT is the same
as that of the tourer, but the GT has slightly stronger rear springs
and front springs of a slightly different static length.

The braking system

The braking system is Lockheed hydraulically-operated, with
disc brakes on the front and drum brakes on the rear.

The rear drum brakes are of the leading and trailing shoe
type, each wheel unit being operated by a single hydraulic cylinder.
Equal braking is obtained whether the car is being driven forwards
or backwards.

Adjustment of the shoe-to-drum clearance is by an adjuster at
the top inner side of each brake back-plate.

The handbrake is cable operated and works on each pair of
brake shoes through a lever compensator.

The front disc callipers are retained on the swivel axle by two
special bolts, each calliper holding two friction pads, each of which is
retained on its respective side of the disc by a pair of springs and pins.

Each calliper is manufactured in two halves, the attachment
section and the rim section. These are held together by three bolts.
Each section houses a self-adjusting fluid-sealed, hydraulic piston,
dust seal and seal retainer.

When fluid pressure from the master cylinder enters the mounting half of the calliper it passes through internal ports into the rim
half. Even pressure is therefore exerted on each hydraulic piston,
consequently they move both friction pads into contact with the
disc simultaneously and maintain an equal pressure.

CHAPTER 3

A MAJOR OVERHAUL OF THE ENGINE

When any specific trouble occurs with an engine, such as excessive oil consumption, and the unit has a high mileage to its credit, it is often best to do a complete engine overhaul rather than settling for a more temporary repair.

A certain amount of engine renovation can be carried out with the power unit *in situ*, but for major overhauls and the more serious form of competition tuning it is necessary to remove the unit from the car. One of two methods can be adopted, the first being to remove the engine and gearbox as a complete unit; providing suitable lifting facilities are available, it comes out easily. The alternative method is to remove the engine, leaving the gearbox in the car and, where lifting gear is at a premium and the engine has to be manhandled, there is little choice but to do it this way. Whenever possible, however, particularly on early cars, it is best to use the former method, as this lessens the risk of damaging the rather vulnerable straps which retain the clutch-release plate. On later cars the release plate is held in a different manner and there is little risk of damage.

Tools for the job

When overhauling an engine, tuning for rallying or racing, or, indeed, carrying out work of quite a minor nature, a set of mechanics' tools is essential. The basic needs are a large and small screwdriver, a pair of pliers, and set of open-ended spanners, ring spanners, and socket spanners comprising all A F sizes up to 1 in.

A comprehensive range of special tools for specific purposes is available for the MGB, but while they cut down the time spent on a job and tend to make it easier, few of the tools are actually indispensable. A little initiative and mechanical aptitude allow most jobs to be tackled satisfactorily, but the minimum requirements as regards special tools for an engine overhaul are a torque wrench, circlip pliers, a valve-spring compressor, a piston-ring compressor, and a clutch-alignment mandrel.

Removing the engine

Before major work of any kind is started, always disconnect the battery. When this has been done the oil and water may be drained and the bonnet removed.

If an oil cooler is fitted, disconnect the pipes from the engine and remove the support which is attached to the dynamo bracket. After disconnecting the water hoses, remove the bolts which secure the radiator support tie-bars, take out the diaphragm-to-body bolts, disconnect the pipes from the oil cooler and lift the assembly out complete.

The air cleaners, carburetters and heat shield may now be removed. Afterwards disconnect the exhaust-pipe flange, and remove the inlet and exhaust manifolds.

Disconnect and remove the coil and its mounting bracket. Remove the bolts from the front engine mountings and disconnect the thermal transmitter, oil-pressure pipe, heater-control cable and the two heater hoses. Remove the oil-filter body, the starter motor, and the distributor cap with the plug leads attached.

Attach two B.M.C. engine-lifting eye brackets to the rocker cover by fitting them between the rocker cover sealing rubbers and the retaining nuts. Place a chain of approximately 18 in. length between the eye brackets and attach the lifting equipment. The slack in the chain will be taken up as the engine is lifted but still allow the engine to be tilted to the required angle.

If the engine is being removed without the gearbox, support the gearbox with a jack and remove the nuts and bolts which secure the gearbox/clutch housing to the rear engine-mounting plate. Subsequently, tie the exhaust-pipe bracket to one side, otherwise it will get in the way.

When all is ready, raise the engine slightly and pull the engine forward until the clutch is free from the gearbox first-motion shaft. On early cars it is important at this stage to take care not to place any undue load on the clutch-release-plate drive straps.

Continue lifting the engine slowly, tilting it up at the front to allow the sump to clear the front cross-member. Once clear of the cross-member pull the engine further forward, when it will come clear of the first-motion shaft and can be lifted out.

If the engine and gearbox are being taken out as a complete unit, do not, of course, remove the bolts securing the clutch housing to the engine plate, but remove the propeller shaft, first marking both of the flanges at each end with a light dab of paint to ensure that the propeller shaft can be replaced in exactly the same position.

Disconnect the speedo cable. Remove the clutch slave cylinder and tie it to one side, but do not undo the hydraulic pipe. Subsequently, remove the pushrod from the clutch withdrawal lever.

Remove the rear cross-member retaining bolts and allow the weight of the engine to be taken by the fixed body cross-member. Disconnect the engine stayrod from the gearbox (if fitted) and the four nuts securing the cross-member to the rear gearbox-mounting rubbers. Withdraw the rear cross-member and put it to one side for cleaning and examination.

Remove the rubber cover from the gearbox tunnel and take out the gear lever, lifting it vertically so as to retain the nylon cup on the end. On cars fitted with overdrive the gear-lever remote control must be removed and the electrical wires to the overdrive disconnected. To do this, the radio speaker panel must be removed by taking out the four retaining screws and removing the remote control cover, subsequently pulling the solenoid wire from the snap connector and disconnecting the gear switch wires. The remote control is held by four bolts. When these have been taken out the control unit can be lifted upwards and out, but may need a slight tap with a hide mallet to break the joint.

The B.M.C. lifting eyes must now be attached as suggested on page 19 so as to allow the engine to be tipped to a fairly acute angle. Before attempting to remove the unit, however, first check to ensure that nothing has been overlooked, particularly wires and controls for any auxiliary equipment that has been added to the car.

Dismantling the engine

The first procedure is to remove the gearbox, distributor body and all external accessories, including the dynamo and water pump. If a 'GF' series engine is being overhauled, the exhaust-emission control equipment should also be taken off.

On high-mileage cars, set these units aside for possible overhaul.

During all dismantling procedure it is wise to keep all nuts and bolts in a box, or tray, which is divided into various compartments. This saves a considerable amount of time and exasperation when rebuilding.

Tap up the lockwasher on the crankshaft pulley retaining bolt and remove the bolt, using a socket spanner or the shock-type spanner 18G 98.

Tool 18G 2 will remove the pulley better than tyre levers and avoid damage to the timing covers.

When the timing cover has been removed take the plug from the bottom of the chain tensioner, insert an $\frac{1}{8}$ in. Allen key and turn clockwise until the rubber slipper head is fully retracted and locked behind the limiting peg. The chain tensioner may now be removed complete by tapping the lockwasher back and undoing the two retaining bolts.

The next step is to unlock and remove the camshaft chainwheel nut, subsequently levering the camshaft and crankshaft chain wheels forward. Ease each wheel a fraction at a time. On high mileage engines they can be quite tight, but two small tyre levers and a little persistence usually do the trick.

After the camshaft retaining plate and the engine bearer plate have been removed, attention can be given to the rear end to remove the clutch, flywheel and engine-mounting plate. These are straight-forward operations, but the tyre levers may be needed again to assist in loosening the flywheel.

The next step is to remove the cylinder head. To do this take off the valve cover and subsequently remove the four rocker bracket fixing nuts. Take them off gradually, in conjunction with the cylinder-head nuts, undoing them a turn at a time in the sequence depicted in fig. 3:1 until the load on the nuts is released.

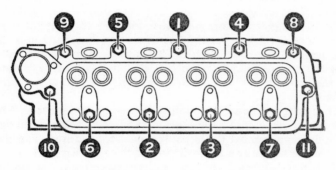

Fig. 3:1. Cylinder head nut slackening and tightening sequence

Note the locking plate, on the right-hand rear rocker-post nut, for replacement in the same position when reassembling. Lift off the rocker assembly, take off the two side plates and withdraw the push rods and cam followers, keeping both the rods and cam followers in the correct sequence, unless they are to be renewed.

When the ignition vacuum-pipe bracket and the pipe have been removed from the rear cylinder-head stud, lift the head off, lifting evenly with a direct pull. Should the head prove tight, break the joint by giving a light tap on each side of the head with a hide mallet, or a hammer with a piece of wood interposed.

When the head has been lifted off, the distributor shank housing and drive shaft should be removed. To do this, remove the securing bolt and pull the housing from the cylinder block. Next screw a 3 in. × $\frac{5}{16}$ in. UNF bolt into the thread in the drive-shaft head. The shaft may now be lifted out with the bolt, but on 18GB, 18GD and 18GF engines it will be necessary to have nos. 1 and 4 pistons halfway up the bores, otherwise the crankshaft will obstruct the drive shaft, preventing it from being withdrawn.

The next step is to withdraw the cylinder-head studs, using either an extractor tool or by locking two nuts together on the thread of each stud and using a suitably-sized spanner on the bottom nut.

After removal of the cylinder-head studs the engine should be turned upside down for removal of the sump. When the engine is being upended, place a wooden board under the face of the block to avoid scratch marks and other damage.

After the sump has been removed, unscrew the oil-pump retaining nuts, and withdraw the pump complete with the oil strainer and drive shaft.

The camshaft may now be removed and the pistons and connecting rods taken out. When doing this it is best to place the cylinder block on its side.

It is essential to store any parts that are to be refitted to the engine in their relative positions to avoid any likelihood of mistake. With pistons and connecting-rod assemblies it is a sound idea to mark the cylinder numbers on the left-hand side of both the rod and the cap whilst they are in the engine if they are not already marked.

Turn the engine so that connecting rods 1 and 4 are at bottom dead centre and remove the big-end caps. Push the pistons up the bore a little and remove the upper big-end shell bearings. The pistons may now be withdrawn from the top of the cylinder block, the caps and bearings then being replaced on their respective connecting rods.

It is entirely dependent upon the wear of the cylinder bores as to how easily the pistons and con-rods come out of the block. On high-mileage units there will be a distinct ridge at the top of the bore where the rings do not reach; in this case a fairly hefty push with a hammer shaft is the easiest method.

When all four pistons and con-rods have been removed the main bearing caps may be marked to aid correct replacement and the self-lock nuts undone and the caps removed. The front and rear caps will probably be somewhat tight, but although tool no. 18G 42A and the adaptor 18G 42C are a help they are not essential.

The centre main-bearing cap retains the bottom halves of the two crankshaft thrust-washers and it is important to note which 'faces' go against the cap, as wrongly replaced thrust-washers can cause the engine to be ruined after a few hundred miles.

Having removed the bearing caps, lift the crankshaft from the crankcase, retain the main-bearing shells and the top thrust-washers.

Before any further work is carried out, all parts must be thoroughly cleaned and laid out for inspection and measuring.

Although petrol may be used for cleaning, there are several proprietary cleaning fluids available. Whatever is adopted, a stiff paint brush, plenty of fluid and a good syringe are essential.

Before cleaning the cylinder block, scrape any old gasket material from the sealing faces and remove the oil relief-valve cap, spring and valve from the rear left-hand side of the cylinder block. Clean thoroughly and syringe all oilways in both the block and crankshaft, being extra cautious if the engine has run any bearings.

Whenever an engine is overhauled queries arise regarding the future serviceability of items such as the crankshaft, timing sprocket, or valve guides. Measurement of the components and comparison with the measurements given in the Appendix may help one to reach a decision, but it cannot reveal flaws or fatigue. If any doubt exists regarding the serviceability of any part whatsoever, it pays to play safe and renew or, alternatively, consult your agent. How the engine was performing in the car, of course, gives some indication of what attention is going to be necessary. Plugs oiling up and heavy oil consumption doubtless means a rebore and new pistons and rings. Low oil pressure probably means new bearings and a reground crankshaft and possibly an oil pump.

A light knock, something like a tappet with excessive clearance, probably indicates badly worn cam-followers, but on a high-mileage engine all of these items are best renewed, even if measurements indicate they are not completely unserviceable.

If the crankshaft shows signs of ovality or scoring on main journals or crankpins it is advisable to fit a reground crankshaft with the appropriate bearings. Reground assemblies are available ·020 in., ·030 and ·040 in. undersize. When used with the appropriate bearings of suitable size both the mains and big-ends have a diametrical clearance of ·001 in. to ·0027 in. Part numbers of replacement crankshafts, etc., are given in the Appendix.

If the crankshaft is in fairly good condition give it a thorough cleaning and a careful polish with a 1 in. wide strip of a fine grade of abrasive tape lubricated with oil.

Although some idea of the amount of cylinder-bore wear may be obtained by feeling the ridge at the top of the bore, it is preferable to measure the diameter of the cylinders with an internal micrometer or cylinder-bore gauge. Take the measurement just below the ridge left by the rings and compare it with the measurement taken on the ridge itself. If the difference between the diameters is less than ·005 in. it will be unnecessary to rebore the cylinder block, provided, of course, that the cylinders are not scored or have overheating discoloration patches.

If it is found necessary to have the cylinders rebored, either take the job to a machine shop familiar with the type of work, or to a B.M.C. dealer who should be able to supply suitable pistons. These are available in oversizes of $+\cdot010$ in., $+\cdot020$ in., $+\cdot030$ in., and $+\cdot040$ in. in normal, or low-compression, form. The pistons are marked with the oversize dimensions. A $+\cdot040$ in. piston requires a bore size of 3·20 in., which is an increase of ·040 in. above the standard bore size, the running clearance being allowed for in the manufacture of the pistons.

The pistons are also graded (see Appendix). Usually, unless more than ·006 in. wear is found, the next size of piston will suffice. A cylinder block, for instance, already $+\cdot020$ in. with ·005 in. wear will usually clean up satisfactorily if bored $+\cdot030$ in. oversize.

If the block is to be rebored, the pistons can be removed from the connecting rods and discarded. Where reboring is not being carried out, examine the pistons carefully for scoring marks before deciding to use them again. New piston rings may be fitted, but in this case be sure to have the ridge removed from the top of the bore, otherwise the top ring may foul the ridge with detrimental results. The same applies if new big-end shells are fitted, for they tend to allow the piston extra travel, and if the engine is assembled without removing the ridge a tap may occur.

Although it is possible to chamfer the top ring lightly to avoid the ring contacting the ridge, it is much better to remove the ridge. A special tool is available for the job and any competent machine shop will do it.

On the 18GB and later engines with fully-floating gudgeon pins and bushed connecting rods, before removing the pistons from the rods check the gudgeon pins for lift which will denote excessive wear. To dismantle the pistons from the rods, circlip pliers are necessary to enable the retaining circlips to be removed from the gudgeon-pin bore.

On 18G/18GA engines the connecting rods have clamp bolts in split little-ends, the bolts engaging with a groove in the gudgeon pin. To remove this type of piston, insert a small plug into each end of the gudgeon pin. This will allow the assembly to be held in a vice to undo the clamp bolt (see fig. 3:2). When the bolt has been removed the gudgeon pin can be pushed out using a suitably-sized drift.

When reassembling the pistons on to this type of connecting rod always use new clamp bolts and be sure to line up the groove in the gudgeon pin correctly with the clamp bolt hole in the con-rod, otherwise damage to the clamp bolt threads will result. If the gudgeon pins show signs of wear they should be renewed. This involves a certain amount of selective assembly to get a satisfactory fit. Ideally the pins, when cold, want to be a thumb-push fit for 75% of their

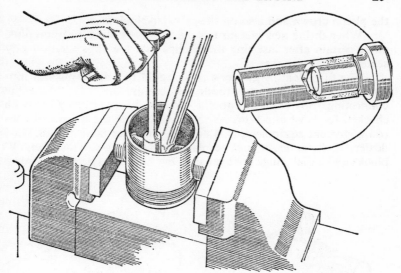

Fig. 3:2. Method of loosening and tightening the gudgeon pin clamp
bolts (18G/18GA)

travel, and yet be sufficiently tight to require lightly tapping with a
rawhide mallet for the remainder of the distance.

New pistons and gudgeon pins are all ready for fitting and only
require cleaning. Lubricate the pins with a little oil when fitting them
and place the pistons the correct way round on the connecting rods.
The pistons are marked 'Front' to assist this.

On 18G/18GA engines it is essential to fit the con-rod and
piston assemblies with the gudgeon-pin clamp bolt towards the
camshaft side of the cylinder block. Renew the spring washer that
goes under the head of each clamp bolt, and if any undue resistance
is felt when screwing up the bolt, remove it, realign and try again.
Tighten the bolts to 25 lb ft with a torque wrench. When doing this,
hold the assembly again in a vice, utilizing plugs inserted in each end
of the gudgeon pin so that undue stress on the con-rod is avoided.

As the 18GB, 18GD and 18GF engines have pistons with fully-
floating gudgeon pins, the connecting rods have bronze bushes in
the 'little-ends' and these must be carefully examined for signs of
wear even if it was impossible to detect any lift. New gudgeon pins
and bushes, however, are not available, and if undue signs of wear
are apparent the complete rod and piston assembly must be replaced.
Oversize pistons for both old and new type engines are available. If
new pistons are fitted be sure to obtain the grade which is marked on

C

the piston crown and also on the cylinder-block face.

When fitting new pistons that have fully-floating gudgeon pins, make certain after inserting the circlips that the clips are correctly seated in their grooves.

The fully-floating gudgeon pins should be a hand-push fit into the rods and pistons at a room temperature of 20°C. Before the connecting rods are fitted to the pistons, however, they must be checked for twist and bow. As this involves the use of special conrod alignment equipment, it is advisable to take them to a B.M.C. dealer. If, however, a surface plate, a suitably-sized mandrel, 'V' blocks and a dial gauge are available, fig. 3:3 shows how to proceed.

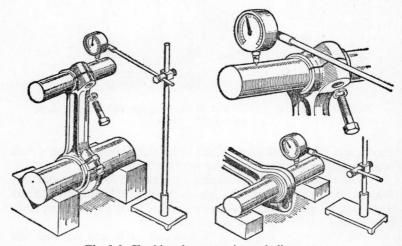

Fig. 3:3. Checking the connecting rod alignment

Should the connecting rods show any indication of twist or bow they must be realigned with a suitable tool.

Piston rings

New piston rings require careful fitting and, even when the new rings are supplied already fitted to the pistons, they should be checked in the bore. The piston-ring side clearance in the grooves is normally correct.

When taking the rings off the piston, remove each ring from the top of the piston, using for preference a ring-expander tool. Failing this, use an old ·015 in. feeler gauge, easing one end of the ring from the groove and inserting the steel feeler between the ring and the piston. Having reached this position, rotate the piston, applying a light upward pressure to the raised part of the ring until it rests on the land above the ring groove. Subsequently, it can be easily slipped off the top of the piston. Needless to say, great care must be taken during this operation, particularly with the scraper rings.

If the pistons are to be used again, carefully clean the grooves and crowns, removing all carbon deposit. When cleaning the grooves do not inadvertently remove any metal from the sides of the grooves, otherwise the rings will have excessive side clearance with a consequent loss of gas tightness, which in extreme cases may even lead to heavy oil consumption.

To check the piston ring gaps it is best to insert a piston in the bore and arrange so that it remains in one position. In this way, as each ring is inserted it will remain square with the bore and a true feeler gauge reading can be obtained (see fig. 3:4). The correct gap

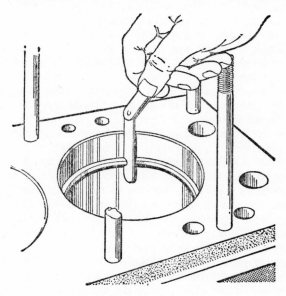

Fig. 3:4. Checking a piston ring gap

is ·012 in. to ·017 in. If any ring gap is found below the minimum clearance, ease the end of the ring with a small file, taking care to file square and evenly.

Rings that are even slightly above the maximum tolerance must be renewed and if new rings are to be fitted to old cylinder bores it is essential to have the ridge at the top of the cylinder removed (see page 24).

When refitting the rings to the pistons, assemble them in the correct order: the top ring is a parallel chrome ring, and the second and third are taper rings which are marked with a 'T' to denote that this face goes upwards, so facilitating correct assembly. Before deciding to use any piston again, carefully examine the skirt, particularly on the thrust face, for any signs of slight seizure or scoring marks, discarding any piston that shows the slightest sign of deterioration.

If the engine has been rebored to the maximum +·040 in. and has more than ·006 wear it will be necessary to have cylinder liners fitted by a B.M.C. dealer.

The cylinder head

The valve springs, cups, cotters and oil seals can be removed from the cylinder head by the use of tool 18G 45. Store the valves and the springs in their relative positions when removed.

Before carrying out any detailed inspection the head should be decarbonized. If special equipment is not available a medium-sized scraper or screwdriver may be used, but take care not to damage the valve seating. Valve ports, and the relief in the top of the exhaust-valve guides, must all be given attention. Valves, too, must have the carbon removed, and all of the 'varnish' must be cleaned off around the valve stems.

After thoroughly cleaning the head and components, check the valve-guide clearance, preferably by inserting a new valve into one of the guides. The correct clearance is ·0015 in. to ·0025 in. on the inlets and ·002 in. to ·003 in. on the exhaust. This is very difficult to determine by mere feel, but due to the oil-seal arrangements, a reasonable amount of wear is acceptable. If in doubt, or if the wear feels excessive, the guides can be replaced, but this will mean the realignment of the valve seats in relation to the guides, which invariably results in the valve seats having to be recut. If the seats are extremely pitted, or exceptionally wide, it may, in any event, be necessary to re-cut them and subsequently reduce their width with suitably-sized cutters. The cost of the cutting tools is considerably more than the charge for having the job done, and it is preferable to take the job to one of the specialist firms or a B.M.C. agent. If valve guides have to be fitted they should be pressed in, rather than be knocked in with a hammer and drift; the latter method usually results in burrs which necessitate the use of a suitably-sized valve-guide reamer.

The tools for cutting the valve seatings are listed in the Appendix, but it is important not to cut the seats more than is absolutely necessary to get a true unpitted seating.

When removing the valve guides, rest the cylinder-head face downwards on a piece of hardwood and press the guides out with a suitably-sized tool made from steel. The dimensions of the tool should be $\frac{9}{16}$ in. × 8 in. with a locating spigot of $\frac{5}{16}$ in. diameter, the spigot being machined to a length of 1 in. to engage the bore of the guide.

Press the new guides in from the top of the head with the same tool, making certain to insert the inlet and exhaust guides in their respective places. Again utilize a press rather than a hammer and be sure to insert the guides with the large chamfer at the top. Press them in until the end of the guide is standing $\frac{5}{8}$ in. above the machined surface of the valve-spring seating (see fig. 3:5.)

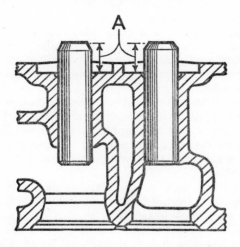

Fig. 3:5. When fitting valve guides they should be pressed in until they are the required height above the machined surface of the valve spring seating. The dimension 'A' must be $\frac{5}{8}$ in.

If a careful inspection of the cylinder-head face reveals that there has been any slight blowing between the cylinder-head combustion spaces, or any distortion is suspected, have the head refaced. The same applies, of course, to the cylinder-block face. As the amount of metal removed is unlikely to be more than ·005 in. from the head and block inclusive, it will make little difference to the compression ratio, for the reduction in combustion-space volume will be offset by the increase due to reseating the valves.

If the valve seats have to be re-cut it is still necessary to lap the valve faces in to their seatings, using a fine- or medium-grade carborundum paste and a suction valve grinder such as tool no.

18G 29. The valves must be refaced first—a job for a local garage—but if any valve shows signs of undue pitting or distortion, and won't clean up satisfactorily, or requires an undue amount of metal removed, it must be renewed. If the engine is being tuned, however, the valves should be renewed rather than be refaced, for the latter tends to reduce the effective valve-spring tension. For normal motoring, however, refacing makes little discernible difference to performance.

When lapping-in the valves, use a minimum of grinding paste (otherwise the paste splashes down the guides), and adopt a quick, semi-rotary action, lifting each valve occasionally to spread the paste and to help avoid 'grooves'. When the job has been completed the valve face and the seat in the cylinder head should be a dull matt even finish, free from pitting.

If new valve guides have been fitted, check the seating with engineers' blue, for it is easy to get a false reading. Rub the blue on to the valve face and, pressing it on to its seating, rotate the valve. Afterwards, examine the seating for the complete circle of blue that indicates all is well.

After completion of the valve-lapping procedure, thoroughly clean the head, again giving particular attention to the ports and guides. Wash the valves thoroughly in petrol, or other cleaning fluid, to ensure the complete removal of grinding paste. After applying oil to the valve seats and guides, refit the valves in their respective locations.

The 18G/18GA engines were fitted with shrouds under the valve caps but they are not fitted to the 18GB, 18GD and 18GF engines. The very early 18G/18GA engines also had valve caps differing from those fitted later.

If the car has done a high mileage, or if the valve seats have been re-cut, it is best to fit new valve springs. Be sure to replace the bottom collars and follow with the inner and outer valve springs, the shrouds if fitted, and the spring caps. Compress the spring, and fit the valve-stem oil-packing ring in the bottom of the cotter groove (see fig 3:6), finally replacing the cotters and removing the compressor.

To inspect the rocker assembly it is best to dismantle it. To do this remove the grub screw in the rear mounting bracket, which locates the rocker shaft, remove the split pin from one end of the shaft and slide off the components.

To facilitate the correct reassembly of the rockers and brackets on to the shaft, place them on the bench in the order in which they are removed.

If inspection of the shaft reveals any wear, renew it. Check the

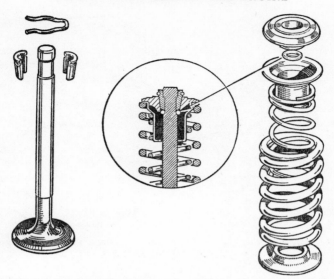

Fig. 3:6. Parts of the valve assembly, showing the valve, cotters, circlip, bottom collar, double valve springs, shroud (early engines only), packing ring, and spring cap. The inset shows the valve packing ring fitted correctly at the bottom of the cotter groove below the cotters

rockers on a new shaft or on a portion of the old shaft where wear has not taken place. If the bushes are worn it is best to fit new rockers, for unless the necessary equipment is available it is not a sound proposition to rebush them.

Oil pump, filter and relief valve

Although the oil pump seldom gives any trouble, it must be thoroughly cleaned and checked for wear. First remove the oil strainer and then detach the oil-pump cover from the main body; this is located by two dowels and secured by two bolts. Then remove the outer rotor and the inner rotor, which is attached to the oil-pump shaft, and thoroughly clean all the parts.

Measure the diametrical clearance between the outer rotor pocket and the pump body with a feeler gauge. If the clearance is more than ·010 in. the pump assembly is best renewed.

The end-float measurements must now be taken by installing the rotor and placing a straight edge or a steel rule across the face of the pump (see fig. 3:7). Measure the clearance between the top face of the rotor and the underside of the straight edge. The clearance must not exceed ·005 in. If it does, remove the two locating dowels and lap the joint face of the pump body until the clearance is less

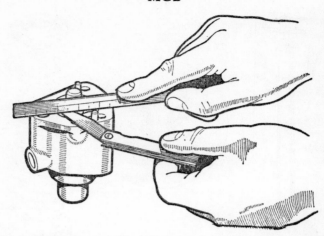

Fig. 3:7. Checking the oil pump rotor end-float, which should not
exceed ·005 in. (·127 mm)

than ·005 in.

Next, with the rotor installed in the pump body, measure the
clearance between the rotor lobes when they are in the position
indicated by fig 3:8. If the clearance is in excess of ·006 in. it is
advisable to renew the rotor.

When it has been confirmed that all the oil-pump parts are up
to standard, reassemble the pump, using clean lubricating oil, and
make sure that the outer rotor in the pump body is installed with the

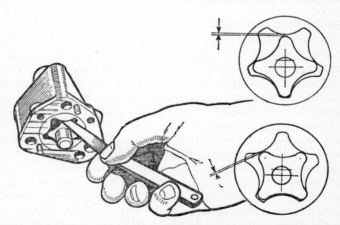

Fig. 3:8. The lobe clearance should not exceed ·006 in. (·152 mm) when
the oil pump rotors are in the positions illustrated

chamfer towards the driving end of the rotor pocket. Don't forget the locating dowels for the oil-pump cover, and fit a new gasket between the oil strainer and the cover.

When replacing the pump in the cylinder block check that the correct gasket has been supplied by ensuring that the oil holes in the gasket line up with the oilways in the cylinder block.

While the engine is stripped, it will pay to examine the filter and modify the assembly as suggested on page 118. On 18G/18GA engines, whilst the oil pump is stripped, the pump cover may be machined as in fig. 3:9 (see also plate 6). On 18GB, 18GD and 18GF engines, however, the oil pump need not be modified unless the engine is to be tuned, or unless constant high revolutions will be used.

The oil relief valve and spring seldom give trouble, but if on examination the valve does not appear to have been seating adequately or wear is visible, it should be renewed. The free length of the spring is normally 3 in. Should it be less, this too must be renewed.

Flywheel and clutch

Although the flywheel starter ring gear has a long life, renew it if worn, otherwise bad starter engagement may occur long before the end of the life of the engine. On high mileage units it is well worth renewing as a precautionary measure, for there is nothing more irritating than a car that gives starter trouble.

The best way of removing the old ring gear is with a cold chisel, taking care not to damage the flywheel.

Before attempting to fit the new starter ring make sure that the surface where the ring fits is clean, removing any burrs or chisel marks with a small file.

The new ring gear must be heated when it will slip on to the flywheel easily. Ideally a thermostatically-controlled furnace is required, but the job can be done without, provided that some heat-resisting fire bricks and a welding torch or blowlamp are available. Place the ring with the lead of the teeth (where the starter engages) facing upwards on the fire bricks. Play the torch around the gear slowly and evenly, removing it occasionally to observe the colour. When sufficiently heated the surface colour turns a light blue and as soon as this condition is observed pick the ring up, using long-handled pliers, and slip it over the flywheel with the starter teeth leads facing away from the register. On no account should the ring gear be heated to any other colour than a light blue, otherwise not only will the temper of the teeth be affected but the ring gear will not shrink sufficiently when cool.

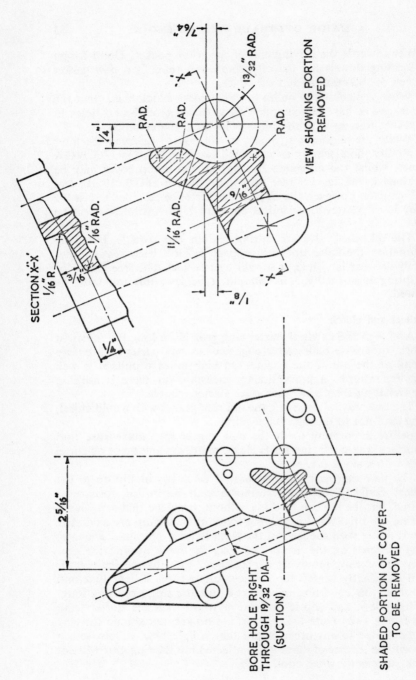

SECTION X-X

1/16 R
1/16" RAD.
3/16"
1/4"

7/64"

13/32 RAD.

RAD.

RAD.

RAD.

1/4"

9/16"

1 1/16" RAD.

1/8"

VIEW SHOWING PORTION REMOVED

BORE HOLE RIGHT THROUGH 19/32" DIA. (SUCTION)

2 5/16"

SHADED PORTION OF COVER TO BE REMOVED

Fig. 3:9. Diagram showing portion of oil pump cover removed
Note: Part of this machining is already incorporated on 18GB engines, but see Plate 6

If the ring does not immediately slip evenly into place, a light tap around the periphery will soon position it correctly. Once the ring gear is in place allow it to cool naturally, the 'shrink fit' is permanent and further treatment is not required.

The diaphragm clutch on later cars has a slightly different method of holding the release plate than the very early models. The earliest-type release plate is retained by a circlip, allowing the plate to be removed from the cover. On later models the release plate (second type) is an annular thrust ring fixed to the cover by a three-legged strap drive which is riveted in position, making the cover and release plate an integral unit. The older type is no longer available as a complete service unit, and although service parts are available it is worthwhile fitting the very latest assembly (third type) rather than go to the trouble of overhauling an old type.

Inspect the driven plate for wear and freedom from oil or grease. The friction surfaces should be of a light, highly polished nature with the grain of the material clearly visible. Do not confuse the appearance with the darker glazed surface which is caused by oil finding its way to the facing and subsequently being burnt off to leave a thin highly-polished carbon residue.

If the presence of any oil or oil residue is observed on the clutch facings the source of the oil leak must be found and the trouble rectified. The wear factor on the working faces of the driven plate is about ·001 in. per 1,000 miles under normal operating conditions. A rough approximation of how long the plate will last can therefore be obtained by measuring the depth of material between the retaining rivets and the facing surface. Where a complete engine overhaul is being carried out, however, it is always worthwhile renewing the plate, for not only is wear of the friction material and splines involved but also the torque-reaction springs and seats. A rough check on the springs is to try rotating them with thumb and forefinger, slackness indicating a need for replacement.

If, when the car was being driven, the clutch was chattering or dragging, making smooth gear-changing difficult, yet the friction faces of the driven plate are good, spline wear of the driven plate may have been the cause and the splines should be carefully checked. In most cases of rapid spline wear some form of misalignment is responsible. Usually the fitting of a service clutch assembly and driven plate will cure the trouble, but in severe or persistent cases the 'run out' of the flywheel must be checked when it is bolted in position. Should the 'run out' be more than ·003 in. the cause must be found and the trouble rectified.

Thoroughly clean the clutch-cover assembly and inspect the pressure plate for wear, ridging and surface cracks. Ideally, the surface should be perfectly smooth and free from blue marks. Check the release plate for wear and the straps, if fitted, for damage and tightness. If any doubts exist regarding the assembly's serviceability, fit an exchange unit of the latest type (part no. 13H3935).

The (MY3D) graphite release bearing usually has a surprisingly long life but, if more than 30% worn, it is worth fitting a replacement assembly.

Water pump

To overhaul the water pump, remove the fan hub with a suitable extractor. Then pull the bearing location wire through the hole in the top of the pump body and tap the bearing spindle assembly rearwards from the body.

Take the vane from the bearing spindle using a suitable extractor and remove the seal assembly.

Clean the parts ready for reassembling and the fitment of a new seal. Carefully examine the bearing spindle for excess wear and if the vane, or hub, had any tendency towards slackness on the spindle when they were withdrawn, renew the offending part or parts.

Although reassembling the pump is principally a reversal of the dismantling procedure, when fitting the bearing assembly into the pump body it is important to ensure that the hole in the bearing coincides with the lubricating hole in the body.

When fitting the vanes allow a clearance of ·020 in. to ·030 in. between the vanes and pump body (see fig. 3:10) and fit the fan hub

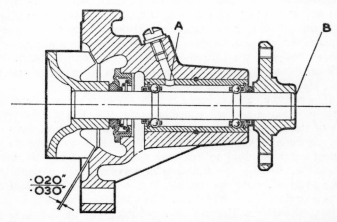

Fig. 3:10. A section through the water pump. When assembled, the hole in the bearing (A) must coincide with the lubricating hole in the water pump, and the face of the hub (B) must be flush with the end of the spindle

so that the front face is flush with the end of the spindle. Take care when pushing, or tapping, the fan hub into position to hold the pump body so that the bearing spindle at the vane end rests on an upright support of a suitable diameter, otherwise the vane clearance will be upset.

Timing chain and tensioner

Clean the components and examine the bore in the adjuster body for ovality; if it is greater than ·003 in. when measured near the mouth of the bore a complete new assembly must be fitted. If, however, the bore is within the limit it is sufficient to fit a new slipper head to the body.

To reassemble the tensioner components (see fig. 3:11) insert one end of the spring into the plunger and place the cylinder on the opposite end. Compress the spring until the cylinder enters the plun-

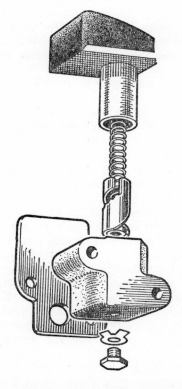

Fig. 3:11. The chain tensioner components

ger bore and engages the helical slot with the peg in the plunger, and with an Allen key turn the cylinder clockwise, until the end of the cylinder is below the peg, and the spring is held compressed. Remove the Allen key.

Now insert the slipper assembly into the tensioner body, replace the back plate, fit the gasket and, with the two set bolts and lockwasher in position, fit the assembly on to the front plate and bend the lockwasher over.

When the timing chain is in place, release the tensioner for operation by inserting the Allen key and turning it clockwise until the slipper head moves forward under spring pressure against the chain. On no account turn the key anti-clockwise or attempt to push the slipper into the chain by the use of force. Remove the Allen key and replace the bottom plug and lock with the tab-washer.

Close inspection of the camshaft may disclose a little wear on the apex of the lobes, but normally on standard camshafts this does not cause undue loss of performance until excessive. Where top performance is required, however, renew the camshaft if the full lift of ·250 in. cannot be obtained. The easiest way to check this is to replace the camshaft in the cylinder block and insert the cam followers.

Camshaft bearings seldom require attention, and only in extreme cases are they likely to need renewal. The work is best entrusted to a B.M.C. dealer with the necessary tools for pressing in the new bearings, as well as the cutters for line-boring them in position.

The timing wheels should next be inspected for wear and any damage that resulted when they were removed. The best way of checking is to compare the old wheels with new ones, but if this proves difficult and the engine has done a high mileage renew them anyway.

Before fitting the camshaft to the engine, if a new shaft is being used, insert the location key and check the camshaft end float (see fig. 3:12) by fitting the camshaft retaining plate and the chain wheel on to the shaft. Tighten the nut and measure, with feeler gauges, the end float between the retaining plate and thrust face of the shaft. If it is more than ·007 in. renew the locating plate.

If a new crankshaft, or camshaft locating plate, or camshaft, is being fitted, it will be necessary to check the alignment of the timing chain wheels (see fig. 3:13). With the crankshaft and the front plate fitted, the camshaft in position and the camshaft retaining plate fitted, refit any alignment shims removed from the old crankshaft behind the timing sprocket and then fit the chain wheels.

When the wheels are in position, check them with a straight edge placed across the face of the camshaft wheel. Measure the

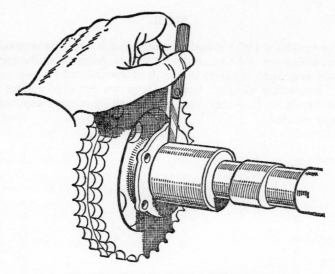

Fig. 3:12. Checking the camshaft end-float

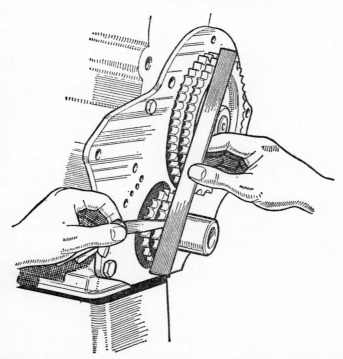

Fig. 3:13. Checking the chain wheel alignment with a straight-edge and feeler gauge

difference, with a feeler gauge, between the face of the crankshaft pulley and the straight edge. Subtract ·005 in. from the measurement and add alignment shims to the value of the resultant figure.

If the timing sprocket location keys are removed during this procedure, be sure to refit them and carefully remove any ragged burrs or suchlike.

CHAPTER 4

REASSEMBLING AND REFITTING THE ENGINE

Before starting to reassemble the engine, clean and inspect all nuts and bolts, replacing those that show any signs of thread deterioration. Renew all spring washers, shakeproof washers and lockwashers.

When all of the engine components are clean, have been inspected, and the necessary new parts and gaskets acquired, reassembly may commence. Adequate bench space and cleanliness are essentials and if the components can be placed in a position where they are ready to hand, and in the sequence in which they will be required, so much the better.

A job that requires doing first, if a new cylinder block is being fitted, is to lap in the oil relief valve with fine carborundum paste, using either tool no. 18G 69 to hold the valve or a wooden shaft that fits tightly into the back of it. After a complete bearing surface is obtained, thoroughly wash the appropriate oilway area, using a syringe and compressed air if necessary.

Whether a three-main-bearing or a five-main-bearing engine is being rebuilt the procedure is much the same. If a new crankshaft is being fitted check that it has a bush to accept the gearbox first-motion shaft spigot in the rear end and, on 18G/18GA engines if the crank is supplied minus the flywheel bolts, insert them before fitting the crankshaft to the crankcase.

Fitting the crankshaft

After checking all oilways, in both the crankshaft and the cylinder block, the crankshaft can be fitted into its bearings in the crankcase. To do this it will be necessary to turn the cylinder block upside down on the bench, standing it on a flat board to avoid damaging the block face.

Insert the thin-wall shell bearings into their housings in the crankcase, taking care that the locating tab on each shell fits into the correct position. Lubricate the bearings with engine oil and carefully lower the crankshaft into position. Slide the top semi-circular thrust-washers into position each side of the centre main, noting that the correct position for the oil grooves in the washers is away from the bearing, the face in which the oil groove is machined going against the crankshaft.

D

Insert the remaining bearing shells into their caps. Place the thrust-washers each side of the centre main-bearing cap and, ascertaining that they are fitted correctly, place the cap on the studs, making sure that it is the correct way round according to the markings.

As a double check, when fitting main bearings and caps, it should be noted that the locating tabs come on the same edge of the housing although on opposite corners.

Fit the remaining bearing caps but, before putting the rear cap into position, coat the joint surface with a sealing compound, taking care not to apply any of the compound too near to the bearing or it may squeeze into the bearing as the cap is tightened. Fit the spring washers, or locking plates, to each bearing cap and screw on the cap retaining nuts and tighten evenly with a torque spanner to 70 lb ft. If the engine is fitted with locking plates, bend them into position. Tighten each cap separately and, after tightening each one, check that the crankshaft spins easily. If it does not, the cause must be investigated and, should the assembly prove correct, with the correct parts fitted, a dimensional check must be made. It is unusual to find causes other than incorrect assembly, or incorrect parts, and normally new parts and service-reconditioned material can be fitted without any trouble whatsoever. Special attention to the thrust-washers may be necessary in the event of oversize thrust washers (·003 in.) being fitted, but unless an old crankshaft is being used the standard washers are suitable and give the necessary end-float.

Refitting the pistons and connecting rods

When the crankshaft is in position, the pistons and con-rods can be fitted, provided, of course, that the ring gaps, etc., have received attention (see page 27).

When fitting these components ensure that they go into the engine the correct way round, and that all marks match up (see fig. 4:1). If they do not, investigate and rectify the cause. Points to watch are that the gudgeon-pin clamp bolts face the camshaft side of the engine (18G/18GA) and that the pistons are fitted to the rods so that the word 'Front', which is marked on the crown of each piston, does in fact face towards the front of the engine.

The connecting rods are offset, and it is essential, if old parts are to be used again, that they are replaced in precisely their original position. If the con-rods and the big-end caps were marked when they were removed from the engine, little difficulty is encountered.

The piston and connecting-rod assemblies have to be inserted from the top of the cylinder block and to do this it is best to lay

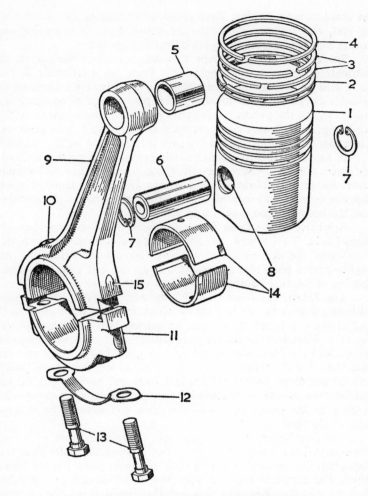

Fig. 4:1. Piston and connecting rod (18GB engine)

1. Piston
2. Piston ring—scraper
3. Piston rings—taper
4. Piston ring—parallel
5. Small-end bush
6. Gudgeon pin
7. Circlip
8. Gudgeon pin lubricating hole

9. Connecting rod
10. Cylinder wall lubricating jet
11. Connecting rod cap
12. Lock washer
13. Bolts
14. Connecting rod bearings
15. Connecting rod and cap marking

the crankcase on its side. Then remove the bearing cap from no. 1 big-end, and insert a shell into the con-rod and the bearing cap, noting that the locating tabs are correctly engaged.

Space the piston-ring gaps equidistant around the piston and lubricate generously with engine oil. Turn the crankshaft so that no. 1 and no. 4 crankpin are at bottom dead centre and check the cylinder bores for cleanliness. Fit the piston-ring compressor tool (18G 55A) to the piston, taking care not to break any rings as they are compressed. Insert no. 1 piston and rod. Give a light push with a hammer shaft and guide the big ends into position on the crankpin.

If any difficulty is encountered, remove the piston and rod, re-tighten the ring compressor and try again, rather than use excessive force. Be sure to lubricate the bearings and fit the connecting-rod cap the correct way round. After fitting the big-end lockwashers and the bolts, torque them up to 35–40 lb ft.

Bend the lockwashers over and check that the crankshaft still turns freely. If all is well, the other rods and pistons can be fitted.

When the con-rods and bearings have been fitted, the rear engine-bearer plate and its gasket can go on, but give the latter a coating of jointing compound on both sides.

The 18GB, 18GD and 18GF rear engine-bearer plate is fitted with an oil seal, the sealing lip of which fits over the flange on the end of the crankshaft to prevent oil getting into the clutch pit (see fig. 2:1). Whenever the bearer plate is disturbed, a new seal should be fitted. Make sure, however, before fitting the bearer plate to lubricate the oil seal on the rubbing lip to avoid any initial seal scorch and do not forget to place the square-sectioned cork (which fits into the bottom of the rear main-bearing cap) into its groove when bolting on the plate, otherwise the plate will have to be removed later to do this.

The rear-bearer plate on the late engines is fitted with lockwashers and these should be tapped over when the bolts have been tightened. The oil-seal retaining plate and lockwasher should also be fitted. The camshaft bearings may now be lubricated and, provided that the end float has been checked, the camshaft may be inserted.

Fit the front engine-bearer plate with its gasket, giving the latter a thin coating of jointing compound, and do not forget the square-sectioned cork which fits at the bottom of the main-bearing cap. Subsequently fit the camshaft retaining plate, using shakeproof washers under the head of each set-bolt.

Setting the valve timing

The timing wheels and timing chain may now be fitted. To do this, and to set the valve timing, turn the engine so that the crank-

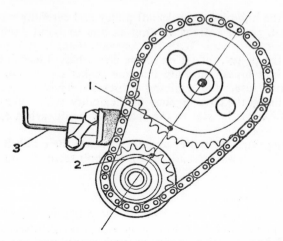

Fig. 4:2. Correct alignment of the timing dimples (1) and (2) when numbers 1/4 pistons are at t d c is essential. The Allen key (3) is used to retract the chain tensioner spring

shaft keyway is at the t d c position, and position the camshaft so that the keyway is at one o'clock when viewed from the front upright position. Now assemble the gears on to the timing chain with the two timing marks opposite to each other as fig. 4:2. Keep the gears in this position and assemble them as a complete unit, engaging the crankshaft timing sprocket keyway with the key until it just starts. Rotate the camshaft slightly until the keyway and key are aligned and push the gears on a little at a time until they are both fully in position. Check that the crankshaft is still exactly on t d c, re-check the timing marks and subsequently fit the camshaft-nut lockwasher, noting the tag which locates in the keyway of the wheel. Fit the nut and tighten securely, bending the lockwasher over.

The next step is to fit the chain tensioner (see page 37).

When the tensioner is in position and locked up, fit the oil thrower to the crankshaft. Two types are used, depending on the type of timing cover. The early-type oil thrower is fitted with the concave side away from the engine and must only be used with the early-type front cover. The later oil thrower is fitted with the face marked 'F' away from the engine and must only be used with the later type of cover.

Before fitting the timing cover, replace the oil seal, using service tool 18G 134 and adaptor 18G 134BD. Coat the timing-cover gasket with jointing compound and place it in position. Apply a little grease to the annular groove of the timing-cover oil seal, lubricate the hub of the crankshaft pulley and carefully push it into the oil seal, giving a slight twisting motion to avoid damaging the lip of the rubber seal. With the keyway aligned, and the timing cover on the pulley, slide it on to the crankshaft. Line up the cover with the bolt holes, checking that the gasket has not moved and subsequently insert the retaining set screws. Tighten up evenly to avoid straining the cover against the flexibility of the oil seal or the centralization of the seal to the shaft may be disturbed and an oil leak will occur.

Having fitted the pulley and cover, insert the crankshaft-pulley bolt with its lockwasher and tighten the bolt securely and bend the lockwasher over.

Fitting the oil pump

While the engine is on its side, the oil-pump retaining studs may be replaced and the oil-pump assembly fitted. Insert the pump drive shaft into the drive tongue, fit the gasket in position, but check to make certain that the alignment of the oil holes in the gasket is correct, for several cases have occurred where the wrong gasket has been supplied, with the result that the oil pressure has been grossly intermittent.

Slide the assembly over the studs and, when it is in position, exert a little pressure on the pump, turning the engine slowly to allow the teeth to mesh with the camshaft. Fit the washers and retaining nuts and tighten to 14 lb ft.

At this juncture it is best to fit the flywheel, for while the sump is off it is much easier to prevent the engine from turning when tightening the retaining nuts.

After making certain that the mating faces of the crankshaft and the flywheel are clean, turn the engine until no. 1 and no. 4 pistons are at t d c and fit the flywheel with the 1/4 markings on the periphery of the flywheel at the top. Fit the locking plate and the nuts and tighten the nuts to 40 lb ft, subsequently bending the lockplate into position against each nut.

If the clutch-cover assembly has been carefully inspected it may now be fitted, using an old first-motion shaft or a suitably-sized mandrel to centralize the driven plate.

When reassembling the clutch, place the driven plate against the flywheel so that the wider portion of the central hub is to the rear of the engine. After locating the cover assembly on the flywheel dowels insert the centralizing tool. Tool 18G 680 can be used on 18G/18GA engines, but tool 18G 1027 will be necessary for later engines. Fit the bolts and tighten gradually, by diametrical selection to 20–25 lb ft. Subsequently remove the centralizing tool.

After methodically checking to ascertain that all bolts are tight, and all lockwashers are bent over, the sump may be fitted. Turn the engine over, crank uppermost, placing the block face on a wooden board to avoid damage. If the cylinder-head studs have not been removed support the engine with wooden blocks, otherwise the studs may get damaged.

Check that the crankcase faces are clean, give the new sump gasket a coating of jointing compound, place the sump in position, insert the retaining set-screws and tighten evenly.

When the sump has been fitted, the engine may be placed in an upright position to fit the cylinder-head retaining studs.

Refitting the cylinder head

Wipe away foreign matter from the block face and fit a new cylinder-head gasket, noting that it is marked 'front' and 'top' to facilitate correct fitment. Do not add grease or jointing compound to the gasket, as it is already coated with a special preparation. Place a liberal amount of oil on the piston crowns and, if the cylinder head is ready, carefully lower it over the studs. Refit the cylinder-head flat washers and nuts except for the four which hold the rocker pedestals. Do not tighten the nuts, however, and be sure to use the correct flat washers, for they are of a different material to normal washers.

After adequately lubricating the cam followers and pushrods they can be fitted. Slacken the locknuts on the rocker arms and turn the adjusting screws to their uppermost position and place the rocker assembly on the retaining studs. Fit the washers and rockershaft lockplate. Replace the nuts and pull them down carefully and evenly, checking that the pushrods are seating correctly.

Finally tighten the cylinder-head nuts to 50 lb ft, pulling the nuts down in the sequence detailed in fig. 3:1. Tighten the rocker-pedestal retaining nuts to 25 lb ft and adjust the tappets with a ·015 in. feeler gauge (see fig. 4:3) using the accompanying table:

Adjust no. 1 rocker with no. 8 valve fully open
,,   ,, 3 ,,   ,,   ,, 6 ,,   ,,   ,,
,,   ,, 5 ,,   ,,   ,, 4 ,,   ,,   ,,
,,   ,, 2 ,,   ,,   ,, 7 ,,   ,,   ,,
,,   ,, 8 ,,   ,,   ,, 1 ,,   ,,   ,,
,,   ,, 6 ,,   ,,   ,, 3 ,,   ,,   ,,
,,   ,, 4 ,,   ,,   ,, 5 ,,   ,,   ,,
,,   ,, 7 ,,   ,,   ,, 2 ,,   ,,   ,,

Before fitting the rocker cover and gasket, fit the side covers and gaskets.

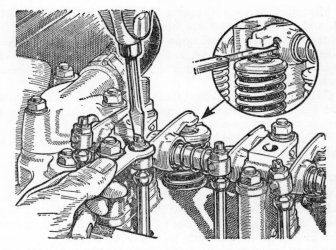

Fig. 4:3. The method of adjusting the valve rocker clearance and the
correct position for measuring it

The next step is to fit the distributor drive spindle, and subsequently the distributor housing and distributor. If the latter has
not been overhauled, this should now be done.

Refitting the distributor drive shaft

The method of inserting the distributor drive of 18GB, 18GD
and 18GF engines is slightly different from that of 18G/18GA
engines.

Dealing with the latter type, turn the engine until no. 1 piston
is at t d c on compression stroke, when the valves on no. 4 cylinder
will be 'rocking', which in effect is when the exhaust valve is just
closing and the inlet valve opening.

Provided that the timing mark on the crankshaft pulley is in
line with the largest pointer on the timing cover, and the valves are
checked, one cannot be wrong.

Obtain a $\frac{5}{16}$ in. UNF bolt $3\frac{1}{2}$ in. long and screw into the
threaded end of the spindle. Hold the spindle with the bolt so that
the distributor locating slot is just below the horizontal but with the
large offset in the uppermost position.

Carefully lower the spindle into position.

As the gear engages it will turn slightly in an anti-clockwise
direction, leaving the slot in the two o'clock position (see fig. 4:4).
Remove the bolt and fit the distributor housing, securing it with
the special bolt and washer, otherwise the bolt head may protrude

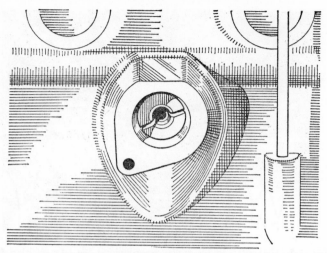

Fig. 4:4. The distributor drive with the slot in the correct position with
the large offset uppermost

above the housing and prevent the distributor from seating
correctly.

With 18GB, GD and GF engines the spindle cannot be inserted
when the crankshaft is in the t d c position and it is necessary to
turn the engine until the crankshaft is approximately 90° b t d c or
90° a t d c before inserting the spindle (utilizing a bolt as suggested
for 18G/18GA engines). When the spindle is engaged turn the
crankshaft until no. 1 piston is on t d c with no. 4 cylinder valves
'rocking'. With the engine set in this manner pull the spindle out
sufficiently for it to clear the camshaft gear and turn it so that the
slot which engages the distributor shaft is just below the horizontal
with the large offset uppermost. Re-engage the gear so that the slot
is in the two o'clock position and fit the distributor housing.

The distributor can now be fitted and the ignition timing set.

Refitting the distributor

With the engine on no. 1 compression stroke, rotate the crankshaft until the notch in the pulley is opposite the appropriate
position on the timing cover (see Appendix for correct distributor
settings).

The long pointer indicates t d c, the next pointer 5° b t d c and
the last pointer 10° b t d c (see fig. 4:5). Set the micro-adjuster on
the distributor to the midway position, slacken the clamp-plate set-
screw, and insert the distributor, turning the rotor arm until the

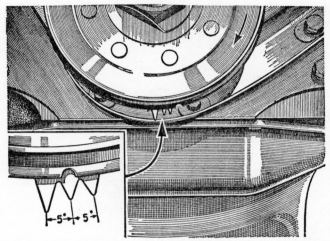

Fig. 4:5. The notch in the pulley approaching the t d c position for
pistons 1 and 4. The inset shows the timing set at 5° b t d c

driving dogs engage the slot of the drive spindle. Check that the
rotor arm is opposite the correct electrode in the distributor cap for
no. 1 cylinder, and position the distributor so that the contact points
are just opening. Insert the two retaining bolts on the clamp plate,
re-check the points, tighten the clamp bolt, and tighten the two
clamp-plate retaining bolts.

While it is possible to get an approximation of the correct
static ignition timing by ensuring that the points are just opening,
it is advisable to carry an additional check with a test lamp connected in parallel with the contact-breaker points.

When the ignition timing has been set, fit the distributor cap
and the spark plugs. Ensure when fitting the HT leads that the firing
sequence of the cylinders is 1, 3, 4, 2.

After fitting the valve cover and gasket, and the distributor
vacuum pipe and clip, the dynamo and starter can now be fitted if
they are in a satisfactory condition.

On 'GF' series engines the exhaust-emission control equipment
should now be refitted.

If the gearbox has been overhauled, and the engine and gearbox
are to be installed as a complete unit, they can now be fitted to the
engine. Take care not to damage the drive straps on the clutch cover
(if fitted) as the box is lifted into position, and after replacing the
gearbox retaining bolts and nuts have a final inspection to ensure
that nothing has been overlooked.

Refitting the engine to the car

Although refitting the engine to the car is basically a reversal of the removal operation (see page 18) a few added tips may come in useful. If, for instance, adequate lifting facilities are available, and the engine and gearbox are being refitted as a complete unit, the oil-filter bottle can be fitted before the engine goes in. This involves a little added manoeuvring when settling the unit into its final position, but it is nevertheless well worthwhile.

Once the power unit is installed, insert the alignment plate between the left-hand-side front engine-mounting bracket and the mounting rubber, before refitting the retaining bolts.

When refitting the propeller shaft ascertain that the flange faces are clean and free from burrs and if for any reason the front of the propshaft has been removed from the splines, reassemble it on to the mainshaft according to fig. 4:6. Failure to ensure that these conditions are met will result in undue propshaft vibration.

Oil grades suitable for the MGB are given in the Appendix.

With 'GF' series engines it is important to ensure that the settings are correct, as given in the tuning data, and that the exhaust is checked on an exhaust-gas analyser.

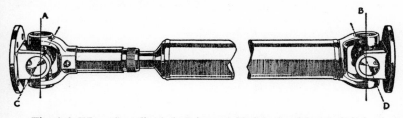

Fig. 4:6. When the splined shaft is assembled to the drive shaft it is essential to see that the forked yokes on both shafts have their axes parallel to each other. In other words, the yoke (A) must be in alignment with the yoke (B), and the flange yoke (C) must be in alignment with the flange yoke (D)

CHAPTER 5

SUSPENSION, STEERING, BRAKES AND TRANSMISSION

If work becomes necessary on the front suspension, most jobs can be carried out without removing the front cross-member from the car; indeed if inspection of the mounting rubbers (see fig. 5:1) reveals that they are in good order it is certainly best to leave the unwieldy cross-member on the car when doing jobs such as overhauling the hubs and swivel axles.

Assuming, however, that it is necessary to remove the cross-member, jack the car to a comfortable working height, and support it by placing suitable stands under the body main side-members, to the rear of the cross-member. Remove the wheels. Take off the steering rack and drain the hydraulic fluid from the brake system (otherwise the fluid may find its way on to the paintwork and cause damage).

Having drained the system, disconnect the hydraulic pipes from

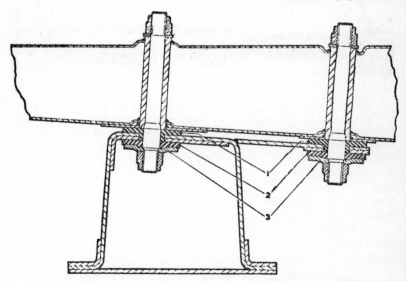

Fig. 5:1. Assembly of front suspension cross-member to body side-member, showing:

1. Upper mounting pad   2. Lower mounting pad   3. Clamp plate

the flexible hose and from the clips on the front-suspension member.

Supporting the cross-member by a suitable jack, remove the nuts and washers from the top of the retaining bolts and lower the unit until it is possible to slide it from the front of the car. Subsequently, remove the bolts and mounting plates, together with the upper and lower rubber mounting pads, from the undersides of the cross-member. If the rubbers are perished or damaged, be sure to renew them before refitting the cross-member. Refitting is basically a reversal of the removal process.

The first step in dismantling the cross-member, once it is out of the car, is to remove the front springs. If the anti-rollbar links have not been removed, this should now be done.

The steering rack

To remove the steering rack, if an anti-rollbar is fitted, disconnect the anti-rollbar links from the spring pan, take off the nuts which retain the steering tie-rods to the steering arm, and remove the arms by the use of tool no. 18G 1063.

The next step is to turn the steering wheel to a suitable position and remove the nut and clamp bolt from the lower end of the universal joint which connects the extended steering rack-pinion shaft to the steering column.

Remove the nuts and bolts securing the steering rack to the suspension cross-member; note that self-locking nuts are fitted to the front retaining bolts. When the bolts have been removed, the steering rack may be pulled downwards from the car. As this is being done, note the packing shims which are riveted in position between the steering rack and steering-rack retaining brackets.

If the same steering rack is to be refitted and the shims are not removed, little difficulty is encountered in realignment of the steering rack, but if a new rack is fitted, or if the cross-member is removed from the car, complete realignment is essential, otherwise steering stiffness, with undue stress and wear, will occur.

The principal task when realigning a steering rack is to ensure that the centre line of the steering column and the centre line of the steering-rack pinion pass through the centre of the universal-joint spider when the assembly is viewed from above and from the side.

If a new steering rack is fitted, or if the car has had overhaul procedures carried out which are likely to affect the front-wheel track, it is important that the track is accurately reset (see page 61).

Steering-rack lubrication

On some very early cars the steering rack is provided with a lubrication nipple. On right-hand-drive cars, access to the nipple can be gained from above the rack on the steering-column side, but on left-hand-drive cars access to the nipple is from below the car. It is essential not to be too liberal with oil and two strokes of the oil gun every 5000 miles usually proves ample, even if a little seepage around the retaining clips of the rubber gaiters on the rack housing is observed. If a bad oil leak occurs, however, the leak, of course, must be rectified and the rack recharged with $\frac{1}{3}$ pint of extreme pressure SAE 90 oil.

On later cars which are not fitted with a lubrication nipple, if the rack has to be recharged with fresh lubricant, this may be carried out by releasing the gaiter from the rack housing (steering-wheel side), turning the steering to the straight-ahead position and injecting $\frac{1}{3}$ pint of the correct grade of oil into the rack. The rubber gaiter must be repositioned quickly, the retaining clip replaced and tightened, and the steering turned from side to side to distribute the oil through the rack housing.

Removing the front springs

The front springs (see fig. 5:2 for all front-suspension components) are best taken off by fitting the spring compressor (tool 18G 693) to the lower wishbone arms.

After adjusting the compressor to take the pressure of the spring, remove the bolts securing the spring pan to the wishbone arms. Release the spring pressure and remove the spring and pan.

If a spring-compressor tool is not available, the springs can be more easily removed before the cross-member is taken out of the car. Assuming that the front of the car is on stands placed under each outer-body side-member, place a suitable piece of wood and a hydraulic jack under the bottom of the spring-retaining pan, and raise the jack to partially take the weight of the car. This will allow the pan retaining nuts and bolts to be removed. Great care is necessary to ensure that the jack does not slip and that the car is firmly on the stands placed under the body frame. The springs may be refitted by the same method, using a $\frac{5}{16}$ in. taper bar to align the bolt holes.

The correct free length of the front springs on the tourer is 9·9 in. If a loss of length of more than $\frac{1}{16}$ in. is apparent they should be renewed.

Removing the front hubs and overhauling the swivel axles

To remove the front hubs, take out the two bolts holding the brake caliper to the swivel axle and so release the caliper. To avoid disconnecting the brake pipes, tie the calliper into such a position that the pipes do not take the strain.

The hubs are retained by a nut and split pin and are covered by a grease-retaining cap. With wire wheels, a little manipulation to remove the split pin which locks the bearing-retaining nut is necessary; this involves working the pin through the access hole which is visible on removing the grease retainer.

After removing the retaining nuts, the hubs may be removed. Unless they have become overheated they usually come off very easily. If difficulty is experienced, two tyre levers or the correct service tool may be used. The tool number for the wire wheel hubs is 18G 363, while for removing disc-wheel hubs the basic tool is 18G 304. The latter must be used with the adapter 18G 304B. There is also an insert no. 18G 304J supplied for this tool, which is required when removing the rear hubs.

When the front hubs have been removed, put them to one side with the wheel bearings, shims and spacers ready for cleaning and inspection (see page 60). Keep the bearings and hubs on their respective sides of the car.

The swivel axles are the next things to remove. Dealing with one side of the car at a time, take off the steering lever, then remove the disc cover, take out the split pin from the upper trunnion pin and the fulcrum pin, remove the nuts and tap out the bolts. Slacken the damper clamp-arm bolt and remove the bolt in the centre of the damper arm, ease the arm outwards just enough to enable the swivel axle to be removed. On no account should the damper arm be completely removed.

Remove the rubber bushes from the upper trunnion link; from the lower end of the swivel pin retain the distance tube, thrust-washer, rubber seals and their supports, and put them by for cleaning and inspection.

Remove the front dampers (see page 60). If the car has sustained any accidental damage, remove the wishbone pivots for examination, otherwise leave them in position and simply remove the wishbone arms by taking out the split pin and removing the nut and washer from each end. Retain the washers, nuts and rubber bushes.

Be sure to keep all parts on their respective sides of the car and after giving all the parts a thorough cleaning, inspect them for cracks and thread deterioration.

All rubber bushes and dust seals are best renewed unless the car is comparatively new.

Release the upper trunnion suspension link, retain the steel and the bronze thrust-washers and lift the swivel axle from the swivel pin. Subsequently remove the dust covers.

After cleaning the swivel axles and pins examine them for wear.

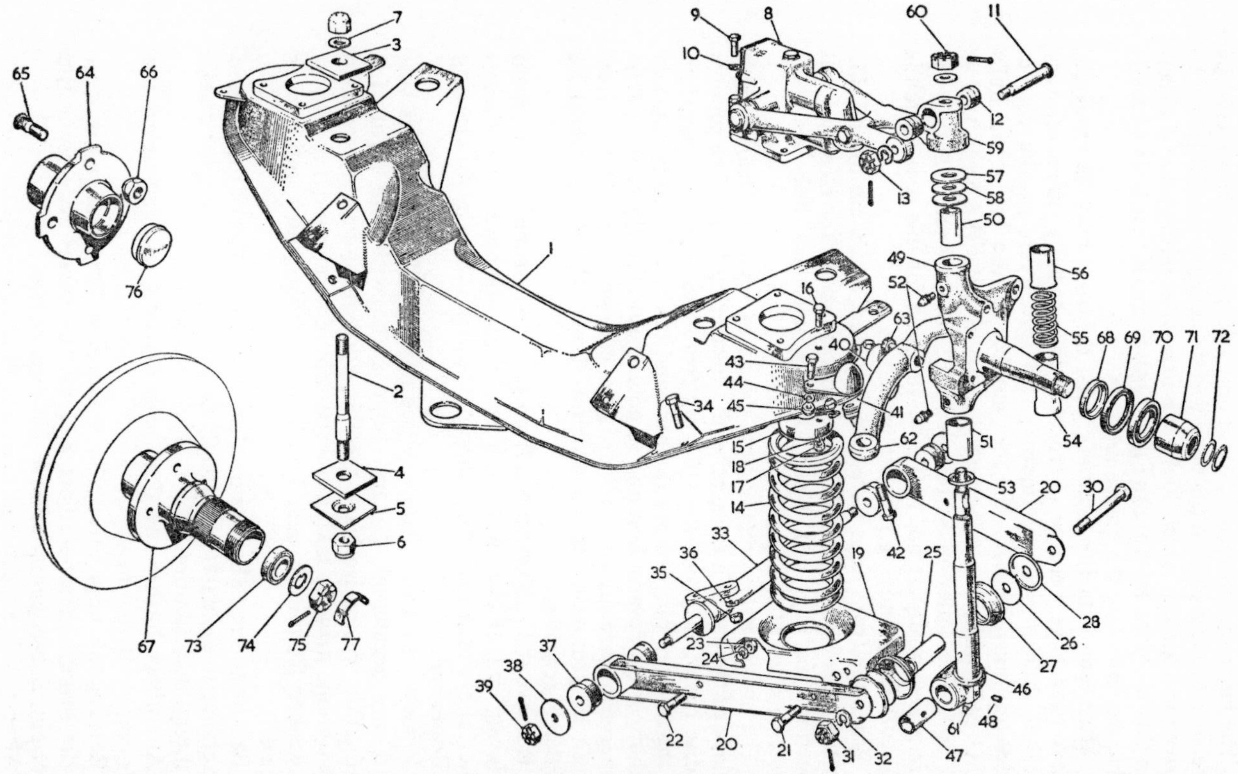

Fig. 5:2. The front suspension components

KEY TO THE FRONT SUSPENSION COMPONENTS

No.	Description
1.	Cross-member
2.	Bolt—cross-member to body
3.	Pad—mounting—upper (rubber)
4.	Pad—mounting—lower (rubber)
5.	Plate—clamp
6.	Nut—mounting bolt
7.	Washer—plain—nut
8.	Absorber—shock
9.	Screw—shock absorber to cross-member
10.	Washer-screw—spring
11.	Pin—fulcrum—top link to shock absorber arm
12.	Bearing—link
13.	Nut—fulcrum pin
14.	Spring—coil
15.	Spigot—spring
16.	Screw—spigot to cross-member
17.	Nut—screw
18.	Washer—spring—nut
19.	Pan assembly—spring
20.	Wishbone assembly—bottom
21.	Screw—spring pan to wishbone
22.	Screw—spring pan to wishbone
23.	Nut—screw
24.	Washer—spring—nut
25.	Tube—distance—link
26.	Washer—thrust—link
27.	Seal—link
28.	Support—link seal
29.	Nut—wishbone pivot
30.	Bolt—wishbone to link
31.	Nut—bolt
32.	Washer—spring—nut
33.	Pivot—wishbone
34.	Bolt—pivot to member
35.	Nut—bolt
36.	Washer—spring—nut
37.	Bush—wishbone
38.	Washer—wishbone pivot
39.	Nut—wishbone pivot
40.	Buffer—rebound
41.	Distance piece
42.	Bolt—rebound buffer to cross-member
43.	Screw—rebound buffer to cross-member
44.	Washer—spring
45.	Nut
46.	Pin—swivel
47.	Bush—swivel pin
48.	Screw—grub—swivel pin
49.	Axle assembly—swivel—R H
50.	Bush—swivel—top
51.	Bush—swivel—bottom
52.	Lubricator—swivel bush
53.	Ring—swivel axle pin (cork)
54.	Tube—dust excluder—bottom
55.	Spring—dust excluder
56.	Tube—dust excluder—top
57.	Washer—thrust
58.	Washer—floating thrust—·052 to ·057 in. (1·32 to 1·44 mm)
59.	Trunnion—suspension link
60.	Nut—swivel axle pin
61.	Lubricator—swivel pin
62.	Lever—steering—R H
63.	Bolt—steering lever to swivel axle
64.	Hub assembly
65.	Stud—wheel
66.	Nut—wheel stud
67.	Hub assembly—R H
68.	Collar—oil seal
69.	Seal—oil
70.	Bearing for hub—inner
71.	Spacer—bearing
72.	Shim—·003 in. (·76 mm)
73.	Bearing—hub—outer
74.	Washer—bearing retaining
75.	Nut—bearing retaining
76.	Cup—grease-retaining
77.	Cup—grease-retaining

E

Place the pin in the swivel axle—it should rotate easily without undue clearance. The amount of wear is more easily discernible if the bottom of the pin can be held in a vice. In cases where excessive wear is apparent in the swivel bushes, the pins and the bushes must be renewed.

(As the fitting of new bushes to the swivel axles entails the use of a suitable line-boring tool, the work is best entrusted to a B.M.C. dealer, who should have the necessary equipment.)

Next, check the distance tube in the bottom of the swivel axle. Should this prove satisfactory, temporarily re-assemble the swivel axle and pin.

When refitting the trunnion adjust it with thrust-washers so as to allow the swivel axle to rotate freely in the pin with a minimum of end play (not more than ·002). Thrust-washers are available in the following sizes: ·052 to ·057, ·058 to ·063, ·064 to ·069.

If new swivel pins and swivel axles are being fitted, or if the old ones are satisfactory, measure the fulcrum-pin distance tubes. They should be 2·337 in. long and ·748 in. diameter; if any undue deviation from these measurements is apparent the parts are best renewed.

Should the fulcrum-pin bush in the swivel pin prove worn, a replacement swivel pin is best obtained. If the fulcrum-pin thrust-washers are ridged and worn, they too will need renewing, but if the faces are flat and parallel and, on measuring, the thickness proves to be between ·065 in. and ·068 in., they may be used again.

If examination of the fulcrum-pin distance tube and washers reveals that they are satisfactory, the bottom fulcrum pin, distance tube thrust-washers, seal supports and seals must be assembled temporarily to check that the swivel-pin end float is between ·008 in. and ·013 in. Any deviation from this measurement should be investigated and corrected.

On later cars, the swivel axles were slightly modified to take an extra grease nipple to enable the lower swivel bush to be adequately lubricated. Early cars can be modified when the swivel axles are dismantled by using a no. 3 drill (·213 in.) and drilling each swivel axle in the position 'X' marked on fig. 5:3. The drilling is in the same position for both axles, the left-hand drilling facing forward and the right hand facing the rear. Tap the holes $\frac{1}{4}$ UNF and $\frac{1}{4}$ in. deep. Take care to remove the drilling fraze from the inside of the axle bush, and remove all drilling swarf prior to reassembly.

While reassembly of the swivel axles is principally a reversal of the dismantling procedure, two things which must not be overlooked are to fit the dust covers and spring to the swivel axle, and to place the cork seal on the swivel pin.

Assemble the swivel pin and fulcrum tube with a light smear of grease but when the job has been completed do not omit to give each assembly a thorough greasing.

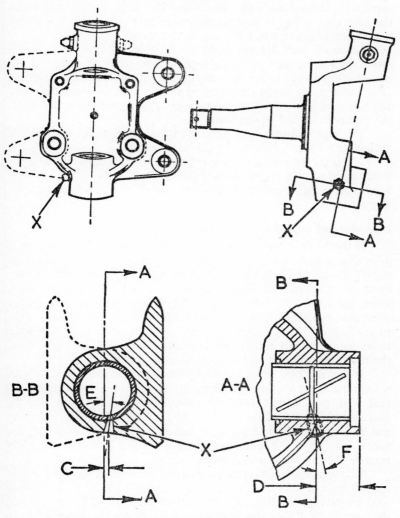

Fig. 5:3. Fitting additional grease nipple to swivel pin lower bush (early cars only)

C. $\frac{1}{16}$ in (1·6 mm)   E. 6°
D. $\frac{3}{4}$ in (19 mm)   F. 12°

Checking the front and rear dampers

The front dampers are retained by four bolts; when the bolts have been taken out and the dampers removed from the car they should be topped up with shock-absorber fluid. Before removing the filler cap, wipe the exterior to ensure that dirt and grit will not inadvertently get in when the cap is unscrewed.

To check each damper, hold the body in a workshop vice and move the arm up and down throughout the complete stroke. If the movement is erratic or free movement of the arm is felt which remains after half a dozen complete pumping actions, or if the dampers show any signs of leaks or if the movement proves exceptionally hard, the dampers should be renewed.

The rear dampers may be given the same examination and, if faulty, they too, of course, should be renewed.

When the dampers have been checked it is not advisable to leave them upside down or to place them on their sides. They must be kept in an upright position at all times and should be refitted as soon as possible.

Renewing and adjusting the front-wheel bearings

If the front hubs are removed during a steering overhaul, or if a harshness develops when the car is cornering, the wheel bearings should always be checked. If they show signs of wear or pitting they must be renewed. The first step towards renewing the bearings, when the hubs have been removed from the car, is to remove the outer and inner bearings complete with the races which are a tight fit in the hub. The bearings come out easily, but the races will have to be removed with a drift and a hammer; indeed, if carefully used the new races may be replaced in the same manner.

When the new races are repositioned, pack the bearings with a high-melting-point grease. Then fit the inner bearing and the oil seal, position the collar (distance piece) and insert the outer bearing and assemble the hub on to the axle. Fit the washer and retaining nut and tighten the nut until the bearings bind. This will pull the races fully against the locating flange in the hub. Subsequently remove the nut, washer and outer bearing.

The bearings must now be adjusted by means of shims to obtain an end float of ·002 to ·004 in. Shims are available in thicknesses of ·003 in. part no. ATB 4240, ·005 in. part no. ATB 4241 and ·010 in. part no. ATB 4242. The best way of adjusting the bearings is to insert sufficient shims to produce excessive end float, noting the thickness of the shims used and tightening the retaining nut to 60 lb ft. Measure the amount of movement with a dial gauge, remove the retaining nut, the washer and the bearing, and reduce the thickness of shims accordingly, to produce the correct end float.

Re-check the measurement with a dial gauge and if all is well finally tighten the hub nut to between 40 lb ft and 70 lb ft. The wide difference is given to enable the split-pin slot in the nut to be aligned with the split-pin hole in the hub.

After fitting the split pin, replace the grease-retaining cap.

If the car is to be used for rallying or racing it will pay to tighten the nut to 70 lb ft and align the split-pin hole by carefully reducing the back of the nut by filing it and rubbing it down on a sheet of emery cloth until the alignment is possible using the correct torque setting. Needless to say, the nut must be carefully cleaned each time it is tried on the stub axle, otherwise foreign matter may get into the bearings.

Adjusting the front-wheel track

On refitting the steering rack or when new king pins have been fitted or if the front-wheel track is suspected of being incorrect (often indicated by the front tyres becoming unevenly worn), steps must be taken to set the track correctly. To do this, an optical alignment gauge, or one of the proprietary instruments for this purpose, is required and it may be best to consult a B.M.C. dealer. If the necessary equipment is to hand, however, the job is quite easy. The track should be adjusted to tow-in $\frac{1}{16}$ to $\frac{3}{32}$ in. (see fig. 5:4), but it is essential to set the tyres to the correct pressure before checking it. The track measurement should be taken in two places; therefore, after the first measurement the car must be pushed forward until the wheels have completed one half-turn. The average of the two measurements must be calculated and the adjustment made accordingly. This may be carried out by slackening the locknuts at the end of each tie-rod, releasing the clips which secure the rubber gaiters to the tie-rods, and then turning each rod the same amount in the desired direction, noting that each tie-rod has a right-hand thread.

It is important that each tie-rod is turned exactly the same amount so that they remain of equal length. The length of the rods can be checked by measuring the amount of thread visible behind each tie-rod locknut.

It will probably be necessary to check the alignment several times and make two or three adjustments before the track is absolutely correct. After each adjustment has been carried out, however, give the steering wheel half a turn in each direction before re-checking the alignment. When the correct average figure is obtained, re-tighten the locknuts and the rack-housing gaiter clips.

On cars where the tie-rods have been adjusted to unequal lengths

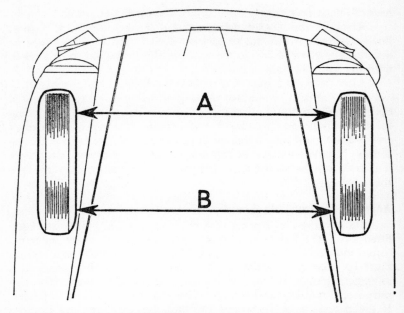

Fig. 5:4. The front wheel alignment check must be taken with the front wheels in the straight-ahead position. Dimension (B) is $\frac{1}{16}$ to $\frac{3}{32}$ in (1·6 to 2·4 mm) greater than (A)

this should be rectified. When this has been carried out it will probably be necessary to realign the steering wheel by removing the wheel from the inner steering column, and replacing it on a more suitable spline, so that the spokes are equal about a horizontal datum line.

Overhauling the brakes

The normal servicing of brakes only entails adjustment of the rear brakes and checking the brake fluid level and this should be done fairly regularly. A major brake overhaul quite apart from attention to the hydraulic system entails the fitting of replacement brake shoes and changing the brake pads. It is important to carry out a regular inspection of the pads every 3000 miles, for although as a rough guide the brake-pad life is 10,000 to 13,000 miles (normal motoring) it is essential to renew the pads before wear reduces the thickness of the friction material to below $\frac{1}{16}$ in.; indeed brake pads should preferably be changed just before the friction material is reduced to a thickness of $\frac{1}{8}$ in.

Apart from attention to the friction material, for complete

brake system safety the manufacturers advise a renewal of all hydraulic seals and flexible brake pipes every three years or 40,000 miles of normal motoring or, alternatively, after every third brake-pad change, whichever comes first. This allows a wide safety margin but a driver who is hard on brakes should not exceed the advised limits, while the car that is used for competition events should have a complete renewal of all rubber seals and hoses after every hard international event.

Brake wheel-cylinder bores and master-cylinder bores also show signs of wear after high mileages and, when replacing hydraulic rubbers, the bores into which these components fit should always be examined. The wear can usually be discerned as a fairly pronounced ridge in the bores. When a ridge is apparent the wheel cylinders and master cylinder should be renewed. The practice of honing the bores and fitting spurious hydraulic rubbers is not recommended.

A brake-pad change entails extracting the pad retaining pins (see fig. 5:5), the spring retainer and removing the friction pads. As

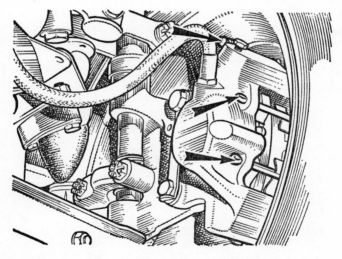

Fig. 5:5. Friction pad retaining pins and bleed screw location

each friction pad is removed, however, a new pad should be fitted.

Before replacing each new pad clean the exposed end of each piston with methylated spirits (petrol must not be used) and ensure that the calliper recess, which accepts the pad, is free from rust and dirt.

Before a pad can be replaced it is necessary to carefully push the calliper piston further back into its bore, using a small clamp or a lever. During this operation the brake-fluid level will rise in the master-cylinder tank and, if the reservoir is fairly full, before starting to fit new pads a little fluid should be siphoned off to prevent it overflowing through the breather hole in the reservoir cap and creating damage to the paintwork.

When replacing brake pads, always ensure that they are free to move easily in the calliper recess and do not bind. If they prove tight, remove the high spots on the pad pressure plate with a file. When all the brake pads have been inserted and the retaining springs and pins fitted, pump the brake pedal several times to re-adjust the calliper pistons. Subsequently top up the master-cylinder reservoir with disc-brake fluid.

If a calliper has to be removed for the renewal of a brake pipe, always refit the correct retaining bolts and tighten them to 40/45 lb ft.

Excessive brake-pedal travel usually indicates that the rear brakes require adjusting. To do this, place the rear of the car on a jack and release the handbrake. Attending to one wheel at a time, turn the adjuster which will be found on the inner top of the back-plate (see fig. 5:6), until the wheel is locked, then slacken the adjuster back one notch so that the wheel rotates freely.

Every 6000 miles, under normal operating conditions, the brake drums should be removed and the brake dust blown out. When

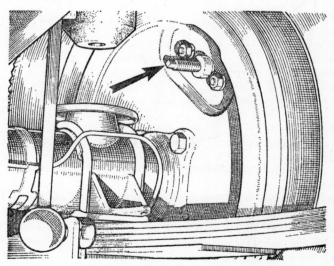

Fig. 5:6. The square head of the brake adjuster spindle

doing this, the rear brake linings should also be inspected, for the rear brake shoes must be renewed before wear of the friction material allows the retaining rivets to score the brake drum.

When the brake shoes need renewing and the brake drum has been removed, using a pair of pliers depress each shoe-steady spring-retaining washer, and turn it to release the washer and spring from the retaining pin. Pull the trailing shoe against the load of the return springs; this will overcome the spring tension and allow each shoe to be removed by disengaging it from the top and bottom locating slot.

As a precautionary measure, when the brake shoes have been removed, to prevent the wheel-cylinder pistons being ejected from their bores, place an elastic band around the slots in the wheel-cylinder pistons where the bottom of each brake shoe locates.

If the piston in the wheel cylinder becomes inadvertently ejected during brake overhaul, refit it and after the new brake shoes have been fitted and the overhaul completed be sure to bleed the system.

Should any leakage be observed from the rear-wheel brake cylinders, the bore of the offending wheel cylinder should be checked for wear. If the bore is ridged, the wheel cylinder on both brake assemblies should be renewed. If wear is not apparent new sealing rubber washers should be fitted to both wheel cylinders. If the dust seals appear to be perished they, too, should be renewed.

When it is not possible to use service replacement brake shoes, the existing shoes will have to be relined. Great care must be taken when doing this and, prior to refitting the shoes, all high spots on the linings must be removed by the careful use of a file. It is essential that all brake linings on the car are of the same make, grade and condition, otherwise uneven braking with disastrous results may occur. The relining of one brake shoe must be avoided, although one shoe will have worn more than its counterpart.

Before refitting the shoes, turn the brake adjuster to the fully off position and blow the dust from the brake drum and back plate. Avoid getting grease or foreign matter on to the linings and ensure that the shoe-retaining springs are replaced in their correct holes in the brake-shoe web. Take particular note when replacing the bottom spring (see fig. 5:7), for if replaced wrongly it will foul the hub and, if nothing worse, will cause a disturbing noise.

Always double check to ensure that the brake shoes are refitted correctly, that the shoes are centralized on the back plate and are located properly in the wheel-cylinder pistons, otherwise difficulty may occur in refitting the brake drum.

When a brake overhaul has been completed, check that the

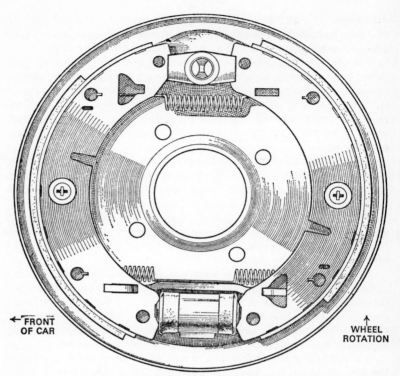

Fig. 5:7. The left hand rear brake assembly

brake pedal does not sink under pressure. If it does sink, this indicates that air has penetrated the system and the system will need bleeding (see 'Bleeding the hydraulic-brake system').

After a brake overhaul the pads and shoes require bedding-in and this may be done by a few careful, but not sudden, brake applications during the first few miles, when a subsequent brake adjustment will give a firmer pedal and satisfactory braking.

If a brake pipe has to be disconnected, or if a new master cylinder is fitted, or if air has in any way penetrated the system, it will be necessary to bleed the hydraulic system before any braking effort can be obtained. Even in the event of the pedal remaining firm, if air penetration is suspected, bleeding should be carried out, for even a tiny air bubble in the system will cause uneven braking which may not be apparent until an emergency arises and maximum braking effort is applied.

The handbrake

The handbrake operates through a lever mounted on the rear axle and produces even braking on both wheels. Although adjustment of the rear brakes automatically adjusts the handbrake, excess movement, due to cable stretch, is corrected by adjustment of the brass nut at the lower end of the handbrake lever below the car floor.

The best way to carry out adjustment is to release the handbrake and, with the rear of the car jacked up, to adjust the rear brakes. When this has been done, apply the handbrake so that it is on three notches and turn the cable nut until the rear wheels are locked. Release the handbrake and check that the brakes do not bind. If they bind, screw the cable nut back until the wheels run free.

If a quick-release handbrake is fitted it may be necessary to adjust the cable a little before the handbrake will remain in the three-notch position.

Bleeding the hydraulic-brake system

It should be noted that the braking system should be completely drained and refilled with new fluid every 18 months. This will involve bleeding the braking system.

To bleed the system a 12 in. length of rubber tube to fit over the bleed nipple is required as well as a clean glass jar to bleed the fluid into and at least 2 pints of disc-brake fluid. This amount of fluid is slightly more than the system accommodates, but the extra fluid is necessary.

Attach the bleed tube to the near-side rear-wheel cylinder bleed screw and immerse the end of the tube in a small quantity of brake fluid. Open the bleeder screw about half a turn. On cars fitted with a dual-type master cylinder, where the back and the front hydraulic circuit is independent, when bleeding the system it is necessary to bleed from a front calliper and a rear-wheel cylinder (on the same side of the car) at the same time.

Top up the master-cylinder fluid reservoir with fluid, and keep it well above the half-filled mark during the bleeding operation, otherwise air will be drawn into the system and another start will have to be made. Ascertain (on single-circuit systems) before bleeding commences that the bleed screw on the offside-rear wheel cylinder and those on the front callipers are tight. (On dual-circuit systems check that both the bleeder screws on the opposite side of the car are tight.)

An assistant will be needed for the bleeding operation; begin by two or three fast strokes of the brake pedal and then depress the pedal slowly through its full stroke and allow it to return on its own. Repeat the slow pumping action several times, allowing a slight pause between each depression of the pedal. Watch the flow of fluid into the glass jar, and when air bubbles cease to appear, close the bleeder screw (or screws), holding the pedal firmly against the floorboards until the bleed screw has been tightened. Repeat the operation on the remaining brake assemblies.

Fluid bled from the system may be used again, but only if it is clean and is allowed to stand for 24 hours until it is completely free from air bubbles.

On completion of the bleeding operation, top up the reservoir to $\frac{1}{4}$ in. below the filler neck and replace the cap. Check the system by applying a normal working load to the pedal for two or three minutes and examine the entire system for leaks. If the pedal feels spongy, or goes to the floorboards, it will be necessary to repeat the complete bleeding operation.

Brake discs

Scored brake discs are not detrimental, provided that the scoring is concentric and not excessive, but heavy or uneven scoring will impair brake efficiency and a new disc (or discs) must be fitted or the offender re-ground. Reground discs, however, should only be resorted to if new discs are unobtainable. If re-grinding takes place, it is important that it is carried out accurately, removing a total of not more than ·040 in. thickness of metal. The amount may be removed by taking off ·020 in. from each side of the disc or by removing ·040 in. thickness from one side only. A total thickness of more than ·040 in. must not be removed and after the discs have been ground the faces must run true to within ·002 in. and be parallel to within ·001 in.

Whether re-ground or new discs are fitted it is important to ensure before fitting them that the faces are absolutely free from burrs. When the discs are in position on the car they should be checked for 'run out' during rotation by a dial indicator. The 'run out' on the periphery of the braking surface must not exceed ·004 in. In the event of this being exceeded, the disc should be removed and repositioned until a more satisfactory measurement is obtained.

Fitting rear-hub bearings and oil seals (cars with a chassis number prefix of GHN3)*

The rear hub bearings are non-adjustable. Should it be necessary to examine them, to fit new bearings or to replace a rear hub oil seal, the rear hub must be removed.

* A few late two-seater cars that have a chassis number prefix of GHN3 were produced with the tubed semi-floating-type axle which had previously only

Assuming that the car has been suitably supported, remove the rear wheels and, if the car is of the disc-wheel type, take out the two Phillips-headed brake-drum-retaining screws. On cars fitted with wire wheels the brake drum is held by four retaining nuts. Make sure that the handbrake is off, slacken the brake adjuster on the brake back plate and remove the brake drum.

The next step is to unscrew the countersunk Phillips-headed screw retaining the axle shaft and withdraw the shaft from the axle case (see fig. 5:8). Note the gasket for renewal and also the rubber

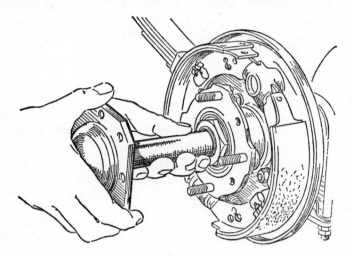

Fig. 5:8. Withdrawing the rear axle shaft after removing the retaining screw

oil-sealing ring. On disc-wheel-type hubs there is also a bearing spacer between the axle-shaft flange and the hub.

To remove the hub, tap back the lockwasher and unscrew the nut, noting that on the left side the nut has a left-hand thread. When the nut has been removed tilt the lockwasher to disengage it from the retaining hole in the axle-case and remove the lockwasher. The hub may now be withdrawn complete with the bearing and oil seal using tool number 18G 304 and 18G 304A (see fig. 5:9).

been used on GT (chassis number prefix GHD3) models. The instructions relate to tourers produced before July 1967. The change to the later axle was made at chassis number 129287 on tourers fitted with wire wheels and at chassis number 132463 on tourers fitted with disc wheels. Where cars have either the same or later chassis numbers the instructions for the GHN4 and GT cars should be followed.

Fig. 5:9. Using Service tool 18G 304 with adaptor 18G 304A to withdraw the hub

To renew the hub oil seal the bearing must be tapped from the
hub with a drift and hammer. The oil seal can be removed in the
same manner, but great care must be exercised when refitting the
seal, and a suitably-sized mandrel is advisable.

When replacing the hub bearing, pack it with grease and,
before refitting the hub to the axle case, give the oil seal a slight
smear of grease.

While re-assembly is merely a reversal of the dismantling
procedure, ensure that the spacer is not forgotten (disc-wheel-type
hubs only) and that the rubber oil-retaining ring is refitted correctly
and a new axle-shaft gasket is used.

Fitting rear-hub bearings and oil seals (G T and GHN4 tourer)

To renew the rear-hub bearings and oil seals on the GT model
and GHN4 tourer the initial procedure of removing the brake drum
is the same as on the early-type tourer. When the brake drum has
been taken off, remove the split pin from the axle-shaft nut, undo the
nut and withdraw the hub. Disconnect the handbrake cable from
the actuating lever at the rear of the back plate and disconnect the
hydraulic pipe from the wheel cylinder.

The next step is to remove the four back-plate retaining bolts
and take off the back plate, removing the oil-seal collar. Take off
the oil-seal housing which is also the hub-bearing retainer cap. If
only the oil seal is being renewed, this may be done without with-

drawing the shaft. Fit the seal with the lip facing inwards and lubricate the seal face to avoid initial seal scorch when the car is first taken on the road.

If the hub bearing is being renewed, withdraw the axle shaft with the impulse extractor tool number 18G 284 and adapter 18G 284D and then press the bearing from the shaft.

Before refitting the bearing to the axle shaft it should be packed with grease.

While reassembly is a reversal of the dismantling procedure, the axle shaft will need careful tapping into position when it has engaged the splines in the differential assembly, moreover the axle nuts must be tightened to a torque figure of 150 lb ft and the brakes subsequently bled (see page 67).

Removing the final drive GHN3 tourer (see also footnote on pages 68 and 69)

To remove the final drive, the car must be placed on suitable supports and have the brake drums and axle shafts removed.

When the oil has been drained and the drain plug refitted and tightened, disconnect the propeller shaft from the rear end by removing the four self-locking nuts and taking out the retaining bolts. Undo the 10 nuts securing the final-drive housing to the axle casing and withdraw the complete final-drive assembly.

Should the assembly prove tight in the casing, a few light taps on the front end, with a hide mallet, will assist in its removal.

Before a new final-drive assembly or service replacement is fitted to the axle casing, ensure that the old gasket is completely removed from the axle casing, and that the new assembly is free from burrs on the fitting face.

Be sure to refill the axle with the correct oil; overfilling must be avoided. As a double safeguard, when the car is on four wheels again, remove the filler plug and allow any surplus oil to drain.

When the car is tested on the road, if any slight propeller-shaft vibration is noticed disconnect the propeller shaft, turn it through 180° and refit, making sure that the fitting faces are free from burrs and that the propeller-shaft retaining nuts and bolts are fully tightened.

Removing the final drive (GT and GHN4 tourer) (see also footnote on pages 68 and 69)

To remove the final drive on the GT and GHN4 tourer it is necessary to remove the complete axle-casing assembly from the car. As special tools are needed when the casing has been removed, renewal of the final drive is best entrusted to a B.M.C. dealer.

Overhauling the gearbox (GHN3 and GHD3 cars)

Removal of the gearbox from the car entails either lifting the engine and gearbox out as a complete unit, or alternatively removing the engine separately and subsequently lifting out the gearbox as an individual unit. If adequate lifting facilities are available, the former method is best. Full details are given on page 18.

Several modifications have been introduced to the 18G/18GA and 18GB gearbox since the MGB first appeared but they are mostly of a minor nature. Only two need be of concern. The first is the introduction of a baulk ring of sintered steel which gives longer second-gear synchromesh life. It must only be used, however, with the new second-speed gear which has a molybdenum-coated synchronizer cone surface.

If the gearbox is being overhauled, or if second-gear synchromesh trouble occurs at any time, it will certainly pay to incorporate the new parts. The new second-speed gear part no. 22H 230 should replace 11G 3064 and the second-speed baulk ring 22H 249 should replace 11G 3063. The change in production was made at engine numbers 18GB–U–H 31472, 18GB–U–L 29123, 18GB–RU–H 31003, and 18GB–RU–L 25995.

The other modifications that may be incorporated relate to the layshaft and layshaft bearings; the latest layshaft is of a larger diameter and the bearings are of a higher-grade material and are caged-type roller bearings instead of uncaged. Fitting them entails a new laygear, thrust-washers and distance tube and reaming the gearbox casing to take the larger layshaft.

The change to a larger layshaft (see fig. 5:10) was first made in production in March 1967 on cars with engine numbers 18GB–U–H 74720, 18GB–U–L 60597, 18GB–RU–H 74529, 18GB–RU–L 58224.

If the gearbox is being dismantled, after making sure the oil

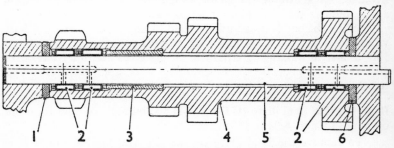

Fig. 5:10. Laygear assembly—second type

1. Thrust washer—small
2. Needle-roller bearing (pair)
3. Distance tube
4. Laygear
5. Layshaft
6. Thrust washer—large

has been drained, remove the clutch-release bearing by rotating the spring-retaining clips 90°. Next remove the nut from the clutch withdrawal-lever bolt (see fig. 5:11 for all gearbox components) and take the lever, together with the rubber dustcover, from the bell housing.

Next, after taking out the dipstick and speedometer drive pinion, remove the propeller-shaft flange (using tool 18G 2 if necessary). Take off the remote-control tower, the gearbox extension cover and the interlock plate and bracket.

Now slacken the locating bolt on the remote-control front selector lever, undo the bolts and the nuts which secure the rear extension to the gearbox and remove the extension by withdrawing it rearwards off the end of the third-motion shaft.

As the extension is withdrawn, the remote-control front selector lever will fall free and should be retained.

When the gear lever was removed (during engine and gearbox removal) if the split nylon bush remained in the selector lever it should be removed and if not damaged or worn it may be placed on the end of the gear lever.

The next step is to remove the gearbox side cover and gasket, noting the fibre washer on one of the bolts for replacement in the same position. This is extremely important, for failure to replace it in the correct position can result in a severe oil leak after a short period of operation.

The next task is to remove the three gear-selection fork-locating screws and take out the two bolts holding the sliding-shaft locating block. A few minutes' intricate manipulation with a very thin-walled ring spanner is necessary, but this allows the selector shafts and block to be removed and refitted as one unit. (If the balls and springs, selector, or shafts require renewing, however, this must be done prior to refitment.)

After removing the bolts, a few light taps with a small hammer allows the block and shafts to be withdrawn from the face of the gearbox; take care to retain the locating pins. If difficulty is experienced, the shafts must be withdrawn separately after removing the wire-locked selectors. They must be removed in the correct order, however, withdrawing first the reverse selector shaft and fork, followed by the fourth- and third-speed shaft, and lastly the second- and first-speed shaft. During this operation the selector balls and springs will be released, so place a piece of rag over the selector block, otherwise the balls will fly in all directions. If the shafts should prove tight, remove the gearbox front cover and lightly tap them out, using a soft drift.

After removing the selector forks and selector shafts, unscrew

F

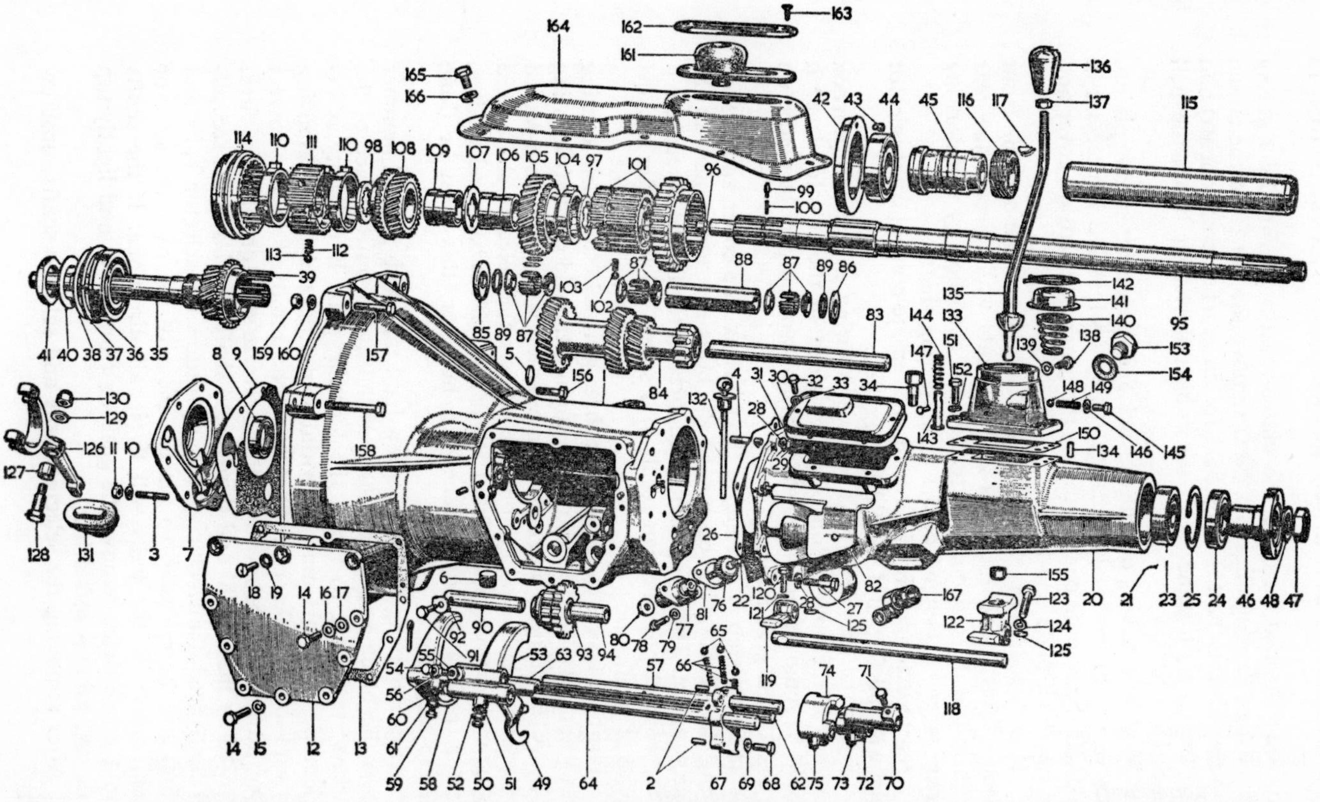

Fig. 5:11. The gearbox components

No.	Description	No.	Description	No.	Description
1.	Casing assembly.	30.	Cover—side—rear extension.	57.	Rod—first and second speed fork.
2.	Dowel—locating block to gearbox.	31.	Joint washer—side cover to extension.	58.	Fork—third and fourth speed.
3.	Stud—front cover.	32.	Screw—side cover to extension.	59.	Screw—fork locating.
4.	Stud—rear extension.	33.	Washer—spring—screw.	60.	Washer—shakeproof—screw.
5.	Plug—welch—casing.	34.	Breather assembly.	61.	Nut—screw—fork locating.
6.	Plug—drain.	35.	Shaft—first motion.	62.	Rod—third and fourth speed fork.
7.	Cover assembly—front.	36.	Bearing.	63.	Distance piece—third and fourth speed fork rod.
8.	Seal—oil.	37.	Ring—spring—bearing.	64.	Rod—reverse fork.
9.	Joint washer—front cover to casing.	38.	Shim—first-motion shaft—·002 in. (·051 mm).	65.	Ball—fork locating.
10.	Washer—spring—stub—front cover to casing.	39.	Roller—needle—first-motion shaft.	66.	Spring—locating ball.
11.	Nut—stud.	40.	Washer—locking—first-motion shaft nut.	67.	Block—sliding shaft locating.
12.	Cover—gearbox side.	41.	Nut—first-motion shaft.	68.	Screw—locating block to gearbox.
13.	Joint washer—side cover to casing.	42.	Housing—rear bearing.	69.	Washer—spring—screw.
14.	Screw—gearbox side cover.	43.	Peg—locating—rear bearing housing.	70.	Selector—first and second gear.
15.	Washer—spring—screw.	44.	Bearing—rear—third-motion shaft.	71.	Screw—selector locating.
16.	Washer—plain—screw.	45.	Distance piece assembly—speedometer gear to rear bearing.	72.	Selector—third and fourth gear.
17.	Washer—fibre—screw.	46.	Flange—third-motion shaft.	73.	Screw—selector locating.
18.	Screw—countersunk—gearbox side cover.	47.	Nut—third-motion shaft flange.	74.	Selector—reverse gear.
19.	Washer—shakeproof—screw.	48.	Washer—spring—nut.	75.	Screw—selector locating.
20.	Extension—rear.	49.	Fork—reverse.	76.	Pinion—speedometer.
21.	Plug—taper—rear extension.	50.	Screw—reverse fork locating.	77.	Bush—speedometer pinion.
22.	Button—thrust—speedometer.	51.	Washer—shakeproof—screw.	78.	Screw—speedometer pinion bush.
23.	Bearing—rear extension.	52.	Nut—screw—fork locating.	79.	Washer—lock—screw.
24.	Seal—oil—rear extension.	53.	Fork—first and second speed.	80.	Seal—oil—speedometer pinion.
25.	Circlip—oil seal.	54.	Screw—fork locating.	81.	Joint washer—speedometer pinion bush.
26.	Joint washer—extension to casing.	55.	Washer—shakeproof—screw.	82.	Arm assembly—interlocking.
27.	Screw—extension to casing.	56.	Nut—screw—fork locating.	83.	Layshaft.
28.	Washer—spring—screw.			84.	Gear unit—layshaft.
29.	Nut—stud—rear extension to casing.			85.	Washer—thrust—front—laygear.

Key to the Gearbox Components—cont.

No.	Description	No.	Description	No.	Description
86.	Washer—thrust—rear—·154 to ·156 in. (3·912 to 3·962 mm).	111.	Synchronizer—third and fourth speed.	138.	Pin—locating—change speed lever.
87.	Roller—needle bearing—layshaft.	112.	Spring—synchronizer ball.	139.	Washer—spring.
88.	Tube—distance—laygear bearing.	113.	Ball—synchronizer.	140.	Spring—change speed lever.
89.	Ring—spring—layshaft.	114.	Coupling—sliding—third and fourth speed.	141.	Cover—ball spring.
90.	Shaft—reverse.	115.	Distance piece—third-motion shaft	142.	Circlip—ball spring cover.
91.	Screw—reverse shaft.	116.	Gear—speedometer.	143.	Plunger—reverse selector.
92.	Washer—locking screw.	117.	Key—speedometer gear.	144.	Spring—reverse plunger.
93.	Gear assembly—reverse.	118.	Shaft—remote-control (rear extension).	145.	Screw—reverse plunger spring.
94.	Bush—reverse gear.	119.	Lever—selector—front.	146.	Washer—spring—screw.
95.	Shaft—third motion.	120.	Screw—selector lever—front.	147.	Pin—locating—reverse plunger.
96.	Restrictor—oil.	121.	Washer—shakeproof—screw.	148.	Ball—reverse plunger.
97.	Washer—thrust—rear—third-motion shaft.	122.	Lever—selector—rear.	149.	Spring—reverse plunger detent.
98.	Washer—thrust—front—·1565 to ·1575 in. (3·962 to 3·9887 mm).	123.	Screw—selector lever—rear.	150.	Gasket—control tower.
99.	Peg—thrust-washer.	124.	Washer—spring—screw.	151.	Screw—tower to extension.
100.	Spring—peg.	125.	Key—selector lever.	152.	Washer—spring—screw.
101.	First speed wheel and synchronizer assembly.	126.	Lever—clutch withdrawal.	153.	Plug—reverse light switch hole.
102.	Ball—synchronizer.	127.	Bush—withdrawal lever.	154.	Joint washer—plug.
103.	Spring—synchronizer ball.	128.	Bolt—clutch withdrawal lever.	155.	Bush—change speed lever.
104.	Baulk ring—second speed gear.	129.	Washer—bolt.	156.	Bolt—gearbox to mounting plate.
105.	Gear—second speed.	130.	Nut—stiff—bolt.	157.	Bolt—gearbox to mounting plate.
106.	Bush—second speed mainshaft gear.	131.	Cover—dust—clutch withdrawal lever.	158.	Bolt—gearbox to mounting plate.
107.	Ring—interlocking—second and third gear bushes.	132.	Indicator—oil level—gearbox.	159.	Nut—bolt.
108.	Gear—third speed.	133.	Tower—remote-control.	160.	Washer—spring—bolt.
109.	Bush—third speed gear.	134.	Dowel—remote-control tower.	161.	Grommet—gear lever.
110.	Baulk ring—third and fourth speed gear.	135.	Lever—change speed.	162.	Retainer—gear lever grommet.
		136.	Knob—change speed lever.	163.	Screw—retainer to cover.
		137.	Locknut—change speed knob.	164.	Cover—gearbox remote-control.
				165.	Screw—cover to tunnel.
				166.	Washer—spring.
				167.	Box—speedometer drive adapter.

the reverse-shaft locating bolt and remove the reverse shaft and gear. If the front cover and gasket have not been removed, undo the retaining nuts and withdraw the cover over the studs. Be sure to retain the first-motion-shaft bearing shims.

Tap the layshaft from the box, allowing the laygear to rest in the bottom of the gearbox. Ease the rear-bearing housing from the rear of the gearbox, withdrawing the whole third-motion shaft assembly. Needle rollers from the front bearing will fall into the bottom of the box during this operation, and should be recovered later and inspected with a view to future use.

The first-motion shaft may now be removed from the front of the box using a soft drift. Then remove the laygear and the thrust-washers from the bottom of the box.

The next step is to slide the third- and fourth-speed synchronizer and coupling (sleeve), together with the baulk rings, off the third-motion shaft, taking care not to withdraw the sleeve from the hub (synchronizer) inadvertently, otherwise the balls and springs may be lost.

Prior to dismantling the third-motion shaft, check the end float on the third-speed mainshaft gear (see fig. 5:12). This will allow the correct thrust-washers to be selected when the cluster is being reassembled.

With a small thin drift, depress the front thrust-washer retaining peg (see fig. 5:13), rotate the washer to align the splines with those of the shaft and remove the washer.

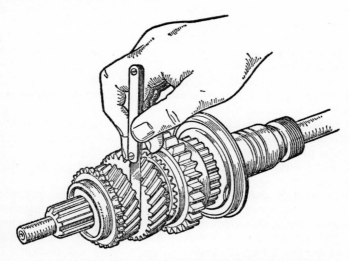

Fig. 5:12. Checking the mainshaft third speed gear end-float

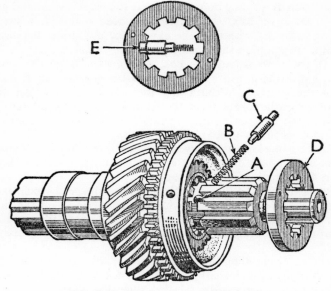

Fig. 5:13. Securing the mainshaft gears

A. Hole for spring   C. Locating peg
B. Spring   D. Locking washer
            E. Peg located in the washer

Remove the third-speed gear, bush, interlock ring and second gear with its baulk ring, bush and thrust-washer.

Next slide the second-speed synchronizer and first-gear assembly from the mainshaft, taking care not to separate the first-speed wheel from the synchronizer.

Remove the speedometer drive gear, the half-moon Woodruff key, and distance piece from the shaft and press off the bearing and housing. If the bearing is to be renewed press it from the housing.

The next task is to clean all the parts thoroughly and examine them for wear, distortion, and general service deterioration. Particular points to watch are: wear on all roller bearings, wear on the clutch-withdrawal lever bushes, and wear on the third-motion shaft bushes and reverse-gear bush.

The layshaft and layshaft bearings usually require renewing even if the car has not done a big mileage. Also examine carefully the first-motion shaft rollers and check the tension of the synchro-mesh springs and the selector-shaft springs. If the box has been stripped for the fitting of close-ratio gears, there will probably be few items to renew, but be sure to renew all gaskets, lockwashers

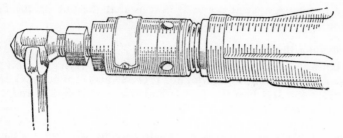

Fig. 5:14. Removing a rear oil seal, using Service tools 18G 389 and 18G 389B

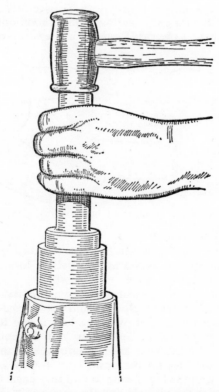

Fig. 5:15. Installing a new rear oil seal, using Service tools 18G 134 and 18G 134N

and oil seals. A special point to note is that the nut on the first-motion shaft has a left-hand thread.

Overhauling the gearbox components

Before re-assembling the gearbox, fit a new bearing and oil seal to the rear extension, using tool no. 18G 389 and tool no. 18G 389B to extract the seal (see fig. 5 : 14) and tool no. 18G 134 and 18G 134N to replace it (see fig. 5: 15).

The front cover should also receive a new oil seal, but when fitting it make sure that it is replaced correctly with the lip facing towards the gearbox. Tools no. 18G 134 with adaptor 18G 134N will facilitate the replacement of the seals but it is possible to manage without them if care is taken.

Assemble the first-speed wheel and the synchronizer (second-speed) and the third- and fourth-speed synchronizer and sliding coupling, using new springs if necessary. Service tools 18G 222 and 18G 223 greatly facilitate the mating of these components, allowing the springs and balls to be fitted quickly and easily (see fig. 5:16).

Fig. 5:16. Assembling a synchromesh hub, using Service tool 18G 222

Assembling the third-motion shaft

Press the rear bearing into its housing and then on to the third-motion shaft. Insert the Woodruff key which locates the speedo gear drive and replace the drive.

Fit the first-gear and second-gear synchromesh assembly to the shaft, followed by the baulk ring and rear thrust-washer. Now fit the second-speed gear bush with the lugs facing to the front of the box and make sure the oil hole aligns with the hole in the shaft.

Fit the second-speed gear and the interlock washer so that the washer engages the lugs on the bush. Now follow with the third-speed gear bush with the lugs facing so that they engage the interlock washer. Check that the oil hole and the cutaway in the bush are in alignment with the holes in the shaft.

Sometimes the bushes are a tight fit and it may be necessary to warm them slightly.

The retaining-pin spring and retaining pin must now be placed in the shaft (see fig. 5:13) and the third-speed gear placed on the bush with the cone facing forward. A very thin drift will be necessary to depress the pin. Position the gear so that the hole in the cone is in line with the retaining peg. Now depress the peg with the drift, fit the thrust-washer on to the shaft and turn it so as to allow the peg to rise and lock the washer in position.

Check the end float of the second- and third-speed gears, and adjust it so that it is between ·004 in. and ·006 in. Thrust-washers are available in four thicknesses as follows:

·1565 to ·1575 in.
·1585 to ·1595 in.
·1605 to ·1615 in.

Position the third- and fourth-speed-gear rear baulk ring, synchromesh hub assembly, and front baulk ring on the shaft, taking care that the synchro assembly is the correct way round.

Assembling the gearbox

The first step in reassembling the gearbox is to assemble the layshaft and laygear temporarily, and adjust the end float so that it is ·002/·003 in. Thrust-washers are available in the following four sizes:

·154 to ·156 in.
·157 to ·159 in.
·160 to ·161 in.
·163 to ·164 in.

When the end float has been adjusted satisfactorily, remove the layshaft but thread a piece of stiff wire through the laygear and thrust-washers, subsequently laying the gear in the bottom of the gearcase. The use of the wire will allow the thrust-washers and laygear to be picked up later and positioned with the taper service tool 18G 471.

The next step is to fit the first-motion-shaft assembly to the gearbox, tapping it carefully into position if necessary. If the third-motion-shaft assembly has been overhauled, place the needle rollers around the spigot of the mainshaft, holding them in position with a little anti-scuffing grease. Now insert the shaft assembly from the rear of the gearbox, placing the gearbox extension gasket in position to align the dowel and the bearing housing.

Take care that the spigot-needle rollers are not displaced as the shaft is inserted into position and make absolutely certain that the bearing housing is positioned correctly, otherwise the rear gearbox housing will not locate on the dowel in the housing correctly.

The layshaft may now be fitted by aligning the laygear with tool 18G 471 (see fig. 5:17). Make sure, however, that the cutaway end of the shaft faces forward.

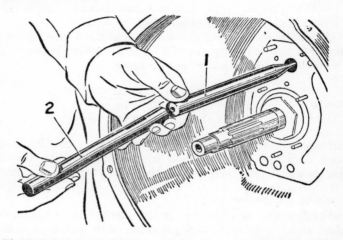

Fig. 5:17. Using tool 18G 471 as a pilot when installing the layshaft

1. Pilot   2. Layshaft

Further assembly is basically a reversal of the dismantling procedure. The main point to watch is that the correct assembly sequence is used. Do not forget to lock the reverse-gear shaft using a new lockwasher and be sure to refit the first-motion shaft bearing shims and align the front cover correctly with the layshaft cutaway. Fit a new oil seal and ensure that the cover fits over the studs easily.

The cover must be absolutely clean and free from burrs and must be centralized, otherwise the oil seal will not be concentric with the first-motion shaft. Apply jointing compound and fit a new gasket to the gearbox front face and then fit the centralizing tool no. 18G 598 to the bore of the cover. Lightly oil the seal and pass the cover over the first-motion shaft, taking care not to damage the knife edge of the seal. Keeping the centralizer firmly in position, push the cover on to the studs. Fit the spring washers and nuts, tightening gradually and evenly by diametrical selection. Remove the centralizing tool.

When securing the selectors to the shafts, be sure to wirelock them and, when positioning the gear-change forks, remember that reverse goes in first, followed by the first- and second-speed, and then the third- and fourth-speed fork. Fit the distance piece to the third- and fourth-speed selector shaft and make certain that the fork-locating screws line up with the shaft holes. Do not forget to tighten the lock nuts and to use new washers. When fitting the gearbox side-plate, ensure that the fibre washer goes on to the correct bolt, otherwise an oil leak will occur.

Before fitting the rear extension with its gasket, place the third-motion-shaft distance piece and speedo gear in position. Be careful, when fitting the extension, that the dowel is lined up, and that the Woodruff key is in position when the front selector lever goes on to the shaft.

Removing and refitting the overdrive (GHN3 and GHD3 cars)

The stripping and overhaul of the gearbox is basically the same when an overdrive is fitted, for the removal of the overdrive merely entails undoing eight nuts. When these are removed from the studs, the unit can be drawn off the third-motion shaft. It is unnecessary to remove the rear flange from the overdrive unit.

If care is exercised in the removal of the overdrive, it can be replaced in the appropriate sequence after the gearbox has been overhauled. It is important not to force the unit, for it goes on easily provided that the planet carrier and the uni-directional clutch are in alignment. The gearbox should be placed in gear and the first-motion shaft turned to and fro to assist in starting the shaft on the splines. Take care, however, that it is the lowest part of the oil-pump cam that contacts the oil-pump plunger otherwise the plunger will be damaged and the unit will not go on.

If any difficulty is encountered when refitting the overdrive, remove the unit and, supporting it in an upright position, insert the dummy shaft 18G 1039 to line up the planet carrier with the uni-directional clutch which lies in the back end of the overdrive unit. If the shaft will not go in use a long thin screwdriver to line up (by eye) the splines in the planet carrier and clutch (turning anti-clockwise only).

When this has been done, insert the dummy shaft to complete the alignment procedure, rotating it slightly as it is fed into the unit. Once the shaft is fully home it may be taken out again and the unit carefully fed on to the gearbox third-motion shaft, taking care once again, as the overdrive and gearbox case come together, that the overdrive oil pump engages the cam correctly.

CHAPTER 6

TUNING FOR ROADWORK

To get the most enjoyment from a car, the first thing is to adjust the seating to obtain a comfortable driving position.

Is your driving seat high enough, or too low for good visibility? Can the steering wheel be turned easily, with each hand able to reach the 12 o'clock position when the seat belts are adjusted correctly? Will it pay to lift the seat a little at the back or adjust the rake? Will extra padding help anywhere? Elementary, yes, but the standard seating accommodation can be tailored to any individual driver's requirement with little effort and virtually no expense.

Pedals, too, can easily be adapted to suit individual needs and may be lengthened by fitting extensions and within certain limits may even be moved to right or left. If 'heeling and toeing' is normally practised, the accelerator pedal may be better modified by the attachment of a small firmly mounted pad.

Perhaps a bucket-type seat is preferred, if so several firms manufacture suitable replacements. If you are not happy with the steering ratio a smaller diameter steering wheel will help (many people find the standard one a bit lorryish).

For increased performance, various stages of engine tune are possible, but remember that tuning may affect the manufacturers' warranty and the authors accept no liability!

For U.K. or Continental owners who do not want to do their own tuning it may be possible to have it done by the Special Tuning Department at Abingdon and, as this department closely liaises with the Competition Department, the latest tuning information, as well as spare parts, are usually available. North American owners should consult either B.M.C./Hambro Inc., Ridgefield, or B.M.C./Canada Ltd., Hamilton (see Appendix).

If any tuning procedure is contemplated, whether for normal road work or competitive purposes, the MGB tuning book available from Abingdon is valuable; six stages of tune are listed, together with information ranging from spark plugs to the fitting of a Weber carburetter.

Tuning the latest GF engine (with exhaust-emission control fitted to American cars), apart from the standard specification given in the Appendix, may result in the car not meeting the requirements of the American clean-air act. It is important that any necessary correction is made to the carburation, etc. The factory or distributor should be consulted for the latest information on this point.

There is little point in tuning a motor car that is well past its prime and if a second-hand MGB has been purchased and the engine is not up to standard performance (see page 90) the cause should be investigated before worrying about tuning.

If the power unit needs overhauling, other things are also likely to be suspect and attention to brakes, suspension and steering must certainly be given. This entails more than a visual check, and with the brakes not only should the friction material be inspected but also the hydraulic system. Suspension rubbers on high-mileage cars often need replacing, while swivel pins and shock absorbers may need renovation.

Insuring the MGB

Generally, extra premiums are not demanded by insurance companies if an MGB is road-tuned and the normal standard parts are retained, so that, for instance, the cylinder head may be polished and the compression ratio raised. But just how far can one go without attracting extra loading?

It depends a great deal on the insurance company, but it must be remembered that in the U.K. the proposer is legally bound to supply all material information concerning his proposal for insurance and this applies to renewals as well. Anyone who tunes his car is legally bound to notify his insurance company. This may or may not result in a higher premium, depending upon the degree of tuning and the record of the proposer, but at least no claim can then be repudiated on the grounds that the car has been tuned.

The cost of insuring a standard MGB in Britain for a 25-year-old driver with a clean record depends on whether the car is garaged in a rural area, or city, and according to the driver's occupation, driving experience and the cover required. For instance, the rates in a rural area in Devon and the rates in Central London can vary by as much as 40%. A full policy for a Midlands rural area with a non-tariff company is £68. On the other hand, an insurance broker's quotation for Guildford, Surrey, for third party, fire and theft only has been as much as £47 with £100 for a comprehensive policy.

Normally premiums for the tourer and the GT version are the same, for although the 'soft-top' is considered the greater risk, the cost of repairing or renewing a GT body is higher.

The cost of insuring an MGB in America for an unmarried, 30-year-old driver, who uses his car for pleasure only, and does not drive more than 10 miles to work each day, and has a clean record, is approximately $100 per year if living in Kentucky (rural area).

In Ridgefield (New Jersey) the same policy costs upwards of an extra $80 per year. In New York City it may cost anything upwards of $300 per year.

The quoted premiums apply to a $20,000/$50,000/$5,000 liability and property policy only. The required coverage is referred to as '5–10–5', or in this case '20–50–5'. The initial figure is the liability for any person injured who is covered for up to $20,000. The second figure is the coverage if two or more people are injured, while the final figure is the coverage for property damage.

Additional coverage, including hospitalization, towing, uninsured motorist (if you are hit by a driver who does not have insurance), collision, etc., is not essential, although the majority of credit companies, banks, etc., who finance automobiles on an extended-payment plan require the buyer to carry some form of collision cover.

American insurance companies consider a great many aspects when insuring a policy, but it is safe to say that owners of sports cars have to pay 10%/50% more than owners of sedans. Special equipment, other than safety items, also make the premiums higher, depending on just what is added, but moderate tuning is usually unpenalized. Many companies have their own innovations and additions to the basic forms of coverage, and as there are nearly 700 firms writing auto insurance, many of them dividing their rates into well over 250 different categories, it is difficult to generalize.

Canadian purchasers of the MGB, if 25 years of age, in the good-risk category may have to pay about $150 per year for public liability and property damage. No significant differentiation exists in Canada between rural and city dwellers, the companies being concerned more with the driver than the car.

Wherever you live do not cut corners when insuring your car—the cheapest policy may prove the most expensive in the long run.

Tuning specifications

The 'B' series engine has a high reserve of strength and road tuning confined to top-half modifications gives excellent results. The modifications may range from a mild stage 1 tune, to the fitting of a flowed and modified cylinder head, such as those marketed by Downton Engineering, which can raise the compression ratio on a standard engine to approximately 10:1. While several firms supply tuning accessories and kits for the MGB, the B.M.C. official stage tuning is excellent, and though stages 1 and 2 produce little gain in b h p they result in an altogether smoother performance.

Stage 1 merely involves polishing the cylinder head and matching the ports.

Stage 2 is the more useful of the two and gives better torque characteristics resulting in improved acceleration in the lower and middle range. Basically, it is a stage 1 tune with the addition of a special camshaft (part no. 48G 184) which has a cam lift of ·216 in.

Although stage 3 of the works tuning procedure is usually regarded as a competition tuning stage and includes polishing the cylinder head, fitting the half-race camshaft (see page 116) and raising the compression ratio to 9·7 by machining $\frac{1}{16}$ in. from the cylinder head and fitting $1\frac{3}{4}$ in. carburetters, it is a fine specification for normal road work *for the enthusiast.*

The stage 3 tune is good even if the standard camshaft is retained, but whether or not the shaft is changed the valve springs, outer part no. C–AHH 7264 (131 lb) and inner 1H 723 (50 lb) will give a slightly extended rev. range and prove better than the 210 lb (total) competition valve springs for road work.

Anyone who wants to go a little further than a stage 3 tune will find that a Downton polished head with a compression ratio 10:5–1 (using flat-top pistons) and with the steel exhaust system and smaller silencer usually produces the desired results. Alternatively, the standard exhaust system may be modified by removing the centre silencer and replacing it with a section of plain pipe.

If a little carburetter noise is not objected to, flared pipes may be used instead of air cleaners, but there will be little gain in power, for they only prove beneficial with a stage 6 tune. Usually the same carburetter needle (SY) gives satisfactory results, whether air cleaners are used or not, provided the light blue springs and ·040 dampers* (part no. 8103) are fitted.

Unless the engine tune is altered more significantly than a basic stage 3 tune, the standard plugs, Champion N9Y, are suitable. If a different make is used, be sure to obtain the correct equivalent.

Brakes

If any substantial increase in engine power is made from standard, some attention to the brakes is advisable, for although the efficiency of the system is high, for regular really high-speed motoring the pedal pressure needed may be too high for some drivers. A brake servo will reduce the pedal pressure, making the car pleasanter to drive at high speeds. A servo kit is available from the Abingdon

---

* A ·040 in. damper allows the carburetter piston to lift ·040 in. before the damper becomes effective. A ·070 in. damper is also available and produces an initially weaker mixture than the ·040 in. damper, for the initial piston lift is higher, thereby causing less depression over the jet which in turn decreases the amount of fuel discharged.

Special Tuning Department and the unit may be installed either on the front bulkhead or on the right-hand-side wing valance.

Undoubtedly power can be a big safety factor if properly used, but to go further than top-half modification (which gives excellent acceleration, good mileage per gallon and an adequate top speed with a wide reliability margin) is unwise unless the car is being used in competitive events and the suspension and dampers as well as the brakes receive attention.

Anyone who likes fast cornering, and does not mind putting up with a harder ride, might prefer to use the competition suspension modifications (see page 128) but, instead of mounting the springs solid, using the standard rubber mounting.

All cars that have been given improved performance, however, should have an anti-roll bar fitted, although it does tend to give a little harshness at the front.

Early cars prior to car no. 11313 had 99 lb/in. (rate at wheel) rear springs, part no. AHH 6453, that did not have plastic interleaving and had plain steel clips without rubbers. If these springs are retained and new front coil springs, part no. AHH 5789, are fitted and used in conjunction with an anti-roll bar the car will have a minimum of roll angle with an added feeling of stability. This specification is also suitable for later cars, but in this case the bump stop rubbers should be substituted for the early-type, part no. AHH 6147.

A very stable car with a low centre of gravity and roll centres does not necessarily have the best handling characteristics for normal motoring. In some circumstances of fast cornering such characteristics can result in a loss of control brought about by the driver being given less time to correct any rear-end breakaway, whereas a car with a slight roll tendency and satisfactory weight transference is likely to have more feel.

The standard front springs (on the tourer) are now part no. AHH 6451 and the rear AHH 7080 (93 lb/in. rate) which have been fitted from car no. 11313. The standard front springs on the GT are no. AHH 5789. Indeed, if the car is not being used for competitive purposes, and is regularly used under all weather conditions for normal road work, the standard suspension fitted with a $\frac{5}{8}$ (standard on GT cars) or $\frac{3}{4}$ anti-roll bar is certainly good. The tourer from car no. 108039 is fitted with a $\frac{9}{16}$ anti-roll bar.

Tyres and wheel balance

Even on a car that has not been tuned but is nevertheless regularly driven at fairly high speeds under varied conditions, tyres are of great importance and the fitting of radial-ply tyres is recommended.

The standard tourer as supplied from the factory is fitted with tubed 560 nylon Dunlop Gold Seal tyres, with SP 41 155 × 14 optional. SP 41 165 × 14 can be fitted on the tourer if desired but only on wire wheels (see also page 109). The GT, however, will take 165 whether fitted with wire or disc wheels.

The initial cost of radial-ply tyres is approximately 25% more than normal cross-ply tyres but is money well spent. On a mileage basis the cost probably works out slightly better, as they have a good wear factor and tend to give a slight increase in m p g. Moreover, radials on the 'B' do not produce any undue harshness or road noise, and as far as road-holding qualities are concerned they are superb.

Whatever tyres are used, keeping the pressures at a suitable setting and maintaining the wheels and tyres in balance contributes to a better handling car. Moreover, less wear is caused, for static unbalance of the front wheels increases rapidly with road speed, leading to certain vertical oscillations of the springs. This in turn results in added wear to springs and tyres, and undue stresses to wheel bearings and dampers; at certain speeds it will be felt on the steering. Dynamic unbalance perhaps is not quite so important at moderate speeds, but it can result in less controllability with wheel shimmy at critical speeds, due to the tendency of the wheels to pivot about the swivel pins.

Road-test figures

The MGB with the 3·909 axle ratio as standard fitment is so geared that in normal top, at maximum rev/min, the car is power-wise at its maximum speed; the use of overdrive (optional extra) reduces the engine revs but does not make the car go faster. If the axle ratio is lowered and the engine is in a high state of tune, over-drive top may be of limited advantage as an extra top gear. On a standard car, in standard tune, overdrive is really for autobahn cruising, its use as a gear to obtain added acceleration being re-stricted to use as an intermediate between normal, third and top. Some drivers prefer their overdrive switch incorporated in the gear-lever knob. Such switches are available from accessory dealers.

To keep a 'B' up to tune, the normal servicing procedures (see page 159) are advisable. If there is any doubt whether a car is up to the normal factory standard, the quickest and best answer is to have it checked on a rolling road. B h p figures can be obtained, but remember this is b h p at the road wheels and not at the flywheel, which is the most usually quoted figure, consequently the peak b h p will be something like 15 b h p less than that quoted by the manu-facturer. Petrol consumption can be tested by a flow meter and elect-

G

ronic diagnosis equipment will quickly reveal any other engine faults.

If the facilities of a rolling road are not available, it is quite easy to test the car on the road to see if it is up to standard. Isolated acceleration road-test figures are by no means completely reliable, as they are susceptible to the varying influences of weather, tyres, road surfaces, etc., but as a snap check the figures on a standard car should be approximately as Table I.

Acceleration through the gears

Speed	Time	
Gear changes at 5500 rev/min	GT	Tourer
0— 60 mile/h	13·2	12·2
0— 70 ,,	16·75	15·9
0— 80 ,,	21·8	21·9
0— 90 ,,	31·5	30·6
0—100 ,,	41·2	38·3

TABLE 1

If the performance figures are not up to these standards, some investigation is necessary. This may result in little more than cleaning and adjusting the contact points, checking the ignition timing, renewing, or cleaning, the plugs and adjusting the carburetters.

If a second-hand car has been purchased, a check with a compression gauge will reveal whether there is much wrong, but before checking, adjust the tappets. Each cylinder should give a pressure reading of 150/160 lb/in², at 300/320 rev/min. Low pressures on one cylinder usually denote poorly-seating or burnt valves or a scored cylinder bore, while if adjacent cylinders at either end are low a deficiency in the head/block sealing may be the cause—probably the gasket.

Should all the pressures be low, this usually denotes general wear, but in practically all cases of low compression the cylinder head must be removed and if the car has not been decarbonized during the previous 15,000 miles this should be done.

In many cases of poor performance the trouble can be traced to a lack of attention to carburetters.

Cleaning and adjusting carburetters

Carburetters should be cleaned regularly. Remember that sticking pistons can give erratic running, stalling at idling speeds and lack of power combined with heavy fuel consumption.

Every three or four months, take off the dash-pots and remove any varnish or carbon deposits from the suction chamber and piston by cleaning in fuel. Remove the damper springs when doing this and be sure to keep the same dash-pot and piston to the appropriate carburetter, and to replace the springs before reassembling.

Always replace the dash-pots in a completely dry condition with just a few spots of thin oil on the piston rod. Be careful at all times not to bend the carburetter needle and, when locating the pistons on to their slides, tighten the dash-pot retaining screws evenly. After reassembly, check to ensure that the pistons are still free and drop back into position. Before replacing the dampers, partially fill the orifice with a thin oil.

Unless the car has done a considerable mileage, or the specification has been changed, any other attention will probably be unnecessary. If the needles are being changed, however, or any engine modifications have been carried out, it will be essential to ensure that the correct needles are fitted and to tune the carburetters. Before doing this, check all engine details which affect performance and require periodic attentions, such as tappets, cleaning and adjusting distributor contact points and ignition timing.

Before starting to tune the carburetters warm the engine up and, after switching off, remove the air cleaners. Subsequently slacken off one of the coupling-lever pinch bolts on the carburetter interconnecting spindle so that each carburetter can be operated separately. Then disconnect the mixture control cable and slacken off the two pinch bolts to free the jet actuating lever.

Screw up the mixture-adjusting nut (see fig. 6:1) on each carburetter to its topmost position and then unscrew both of them 12 flats of the hexagon. (On GF engines only the adjustment within the limits of the jet restrictor is available for tuning.) Unscrew the throttle-adjusting screws until they are just off the stops and then screw them up one turn. Re-start the engine and make any further adjustments necessary to the idling screws to obtain a suitable working tickover speed (800 rev/min).

To synchronize the throttle openings it is best to use a balancing meter. Alternatively, listen to the hiss in the intake, using a length of rubber hose, placing one end of the hose against the ear and the other at the intake. Try each carburetter in turn and adjust the screws until each produces the same intensity of hiss.

When the synchronization is satisfactory, the mixture strength may be adjusted by moving each jet-adjusting nut up or down by the same amount until an even idling speed is obtained (upwards for weakening and downwards for richening) which should give the fastest idling speed consistent with even firing. When this has been

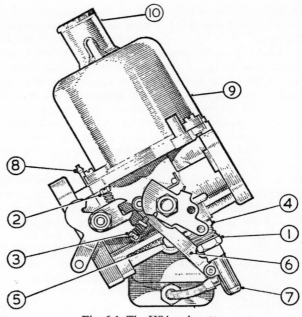

Fig. 6:1. The HS4 carburetter

1. Jet adjusting nut
2. Throttle stop screw
3. Choke or fast-idle screw
4. Jet locking nut
5. Float-chamber securing nut
6. Jet-link
7. Jet head
8. Vacuum ignition take-off
9. Dashpot
10. Damper cap

found it will probably be necessary to lower the idling speed by un-screwing the throttle-adjusting screws on each carburetter an equal amount, subsequently re-checking the hiss from the intakes.

A weak idling mixture gives a 'splashy' irregular type of mis-fire with a colourless exhaust, whilst a rich idling mixture produces a 'rhythmical' or regular misfire with a blackish exhaust.

When the mixture is thought to be nearly correct on both carburetters, lift the piston of the rear one, using the lifting pin on the side of the body. This will produce (a) uneven firing and a decrease in speed due to excessive weakness or (b) an increase in speed denoting richness or (c) a momentarily slight increase in speed, denoting a correct mixture.

Set the rear carburetter accordingly, and make the same check and necessary adjustment to the front carburetter. After each adjustment, check that the jet is firmly against the adjusting nut.

As the carburetters are interdependent, re-check and readjust the rear carburetter. The final position for the adjusting nuts is seldom precisely the same, indeed a difference of two or three flats is quite normal.

Before finally tightening the clamp bolts on the interconnecting rod levers and reconnecting the 'choke' cable, adjust the clearance between the lever pins and the forked lost-motion levers which are attached to each carburetter throttle spindle. To do this, insert a ·012 in. feeler gauge between the throttle-shaft stop and the 'choke' interconnecting rod as per fig. 6:2. Move the throttle-shaft levers

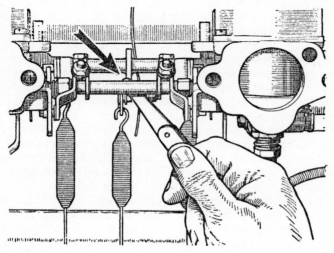

Fig. 6:2. Adjusting the free movement on the throttle interconnecting rod

downwards until their pins rest lightly upon the lower arm of the fork of the lost-motion lever and tighten the levers at this position. Remove the feeler gauge and see that the lever pins have clearance in the forks.

Re-connect the 'choke' cable, checking that the jet-adjusting levers are working correctly and return fully when the cable is pushed fully in. Next pull out the choke and when the linkage is about to move the carburetter jets, adjust the choke/fast-idle adjusting screws to give an engine speed of about 1000 rev/min when hot. Make certain that when the choke is pushed in there is clearance between the fast-idle cam and the abutment screw.

Cars fitted with exhaust-emission control should also be checked on a gas analyser.

CHAPTER 7

COMPETITION DRIVING

'It is difficult to fault the handling of an MGB when it is fully set up for competition.' That sounds like a blurb from the manufacturer's handbook but instead is a quote from an experienced racing driver. His comment highlights the fact that the 'B' is an ideal car for the newcomer to motor sport.

Obviously, under dry-tarmac conditions it is difficult for a 'B' to beat more expensive machinery such as a well-driven Porsche, but the gap is nowhere near so great if it is wet or slippery. Incidentally, the GT version of the 'B' gives more protection in an accident than the open version but its greater weight makes it sluggish for serious competition.

Whatever branch of motor sport you take up, you will need at least two things: a competition licence and a word with your insurers. The only events that won't need a licence are gymkhana exercises, often run for charity, which may involve picking apples out of barrels with your teeth while driving backwards through lines of beer bottles. The sort of competition licence needed for more serious events will depend on the National Club of your particular country; many now sensibly insist on a training period in a certain number of lesser events before the novice is let loose among the big boys.

Increasingly, insurance companies are excluding *any* form of competition, so keep your company informed to avoid unsavoury disputes.

In any branch of the sport, you will drive better if you make sure your seating position is right—and it costs nothing to do this. Short drivers may find that they need strips of wood under the 'B' seat to lift them enough to be able to see the road adequately and 'place' the car properly in relation to it. The 'B' seat is adjustable for rake (a simple spanner job) so with perseverance you should be able to find a relaxed driving position.

Safety belts are essential. They tend to get a bit lost and tangled up behind the front seats but don't let this deter you from using them at all times. For high-speed events you will find a roll-over bar a great comfort (see page 104 for fitting). One or two drivers probably owe their lives to good belts and roll-over bars when they have been involved in serious accidents in the 'B' through over-exuberance (not through any fault of the car, we hasten to add). Lap and diagonal belts appear to be the best in a 'B', although a rally co-driver may prefer a full harness.

Incidentally, it should be possible to reach the ignition switch, when belted in, so that it can be switched off in an emergency. If you can't reach the key, then have an extension piece added to it.

Before dealing with different types of competition let us just point out that however well prepared the car and equipment, you won't *win* without skill and determination but, if cups are not your main concern, you can still have a lot of fun without a great deal of expense or damage to your car.

The following sections deal with aspects of the sport in an ascending order of expense, although this cost grading should not be taken as absolute—it is possible to spend a fortune in order to beat a few other people in a club driving test but there is little satisfaction in winning an event largely because you have the most powerful car. Part of the charm of the 'B' is that it can be very much a giant-killer.

Driving tests

Driving tests or slaloms, as they are called in some countries, can vary from the earlier-mentioned apple-picking antics to full-blooded belts between pylons spaced several hundred yards apart.

They are put first in order of cost because normally they are on smooth ground, which is non car-damaging, and quick reactions from the driver are as important as sheer power; a standard car can win awards in such events if well driven.

A diagram for a driving test may look a complete maze at first sight with lots of to-ing and fro-ing between (and across) lines. Closer examination should, unless the organizer is a complete sadist, reveal a pattern in the test. One test may entail driving forwards into one 'garage' (made up of pylons), reversing into a second, forwards into a third and so on. Others may involve driving forwards over a line, then reversing behind it, then forwards over a second line, then behind it and so on to the end. This is one of the few times when driving tests can be a bit car-damaging if you don't time things properly and select reverse and let out the clutch while the car is still going forwards.

Study the diagram for a test very carefully and, if possible, follow show-jumping practice and walk the course beforehand. As well as the diagram, study the instructions carefully and check whether you have to start at the drop of a flag or in your own time (with the wheels operating an electric timing device) or when a green light appears. Note whether the test ends by stopping astride a line or with a flying finish: the latter is easier to marshal because the timing can end the moment a given part of the car (such as the front wheels) crosses the finish line. The snag with a flying finish is that it may take up more space to run. If you get time, watch the car in front of you go through a test, checking the diagram at the same time to see that it goes the right way round.

Check the marking system carefully—sometimes organizers slip up and put a low penalty for knocking down pylons and then make the test so complicated that it may pay to knock one down deliberately to save time.

The type of tyres you use will depend on the surface of the test area, but unless you are hectically involved in a major driving-test championship you might as well retain your everyday tyres.

The expert test driver will tailor his gear lever so that it is exactly to hand and above all he will make sure that his handbrake works well and preferably is of the fly-off type so that he can perform what are known as 'handbrake turns'. To do one of these, position your hands on the wheel ready to take a handful of lock, then, when the car is moving at a reasonable speed, swing the wheel over, depress the clutch and yank on the handbrake. If you time things well the car should spin round and, by controlling your speed and the effort you put into the handbrake, you should be able to control quite accurately just how many degrees the car turns through. Handbrake turns may be used to spin the car quickly when a test calls for you to go in and out of a 'box' or to go round a pylon some distance away from the rest of the test.

Another technique you will learn by experience is to 'throw' the car when you are going backwards. You will need to do this if, for instance, a test requires you to change direction between one line and another. When you have worked up a reasonable reverse speed, grab a handful of lock and throw the front of the car round. You won't need to use the handbrake but depress the clutch and select first gear while you are whirling round.

Driving tests can be a lot of fun, they are rarely dangerous, they are entertaining for spectators and they are not expensive or car breaking. Incidentally, an overdrive may help with the 'B' on long fast tests by cutting out a few gear changes.

Sprints and hill climbs

Sprints and hill climbs need driving skill but, possibly even more important, they need a certain amount of engine tuning. However, they are not car damaging (unless you go off somewhere) and they are not long enough to take the edge off the tune of a well-prepared car. The only snag with events of this type is that they often entail a lot of hanging about for relatively little competition motoring, particularly in the U.K. where the courses are very short. Even on the Continent, where they have long hill climbs, the running time may only be 10 minutes or so and a driver will be lucky if he gets three runs during a day.

A 'B' owner taking up sprints and hill climbs will need to buy a crash hat and preferably some racing overalls. Most National Clubs lay down strict rules over which crash hats are approved for competition and an efficient scrutineer will throw you out in your own interests if yours doesn't comply; when buying one, therefore, make sure it complies with all the regulations. A noisy exhaust is usually associated with a boy racer, but with the standard 'B' exhaust system you may find it difficult to hear the engine note when wearing a crash hat.

Special clothing

Rapid developments have been taking place recently in the flame-proofing of material for racing garments and it would be wrong to mention specific makes in this book because new break-throughs may have been made by the time the book appears. The only valid advice we can give is that you should obtain the latest information from a neutral body (such as your National Club) before buying anything. Properly-treated overalls are not cheap, but this is not an area for cheeseparing. Have your blood group clearly displayed somewhere, preferably on something which won't burn. Many drivers have their names embroidered on their racing overalls; this at least means that small boys know whether it is worthwhile getting your autograph.

Less necessary but still useful at this stage, are gloves and perhaps racing shoes. With the increasing popularity of leather-covered steering wheels, gloves are no longer quite so critical for actual grip, but they may make you feel more comfortable and professional; psychologically this may improve your performance. High speed driving depends to a great degree on the attitude of mind of the driver and if, for instance, you feel faster with a lucky charm in the car, then by all means carry one.

The sort of shoes you use aren't critical, provided they don't catch in things or restrict heeling and toeing movements.

For sprints at a club level you will probably want to use your normal road tyres, but for more important competitions racing tyres will be faster. You should, of course, throw out your spare wheel and all surplus weight, such as auxiliary lights, etc. Take out the passenger's seat and remove the bumpers if the regulations permit. Whether you leave the hood or hard top in place to improve streamlining will depend on whether you are likely to reach high enough speeds to make it worthwhile carrying their extra weight. If you don't run with the hood up, remove the windscreen as well and fit an aero screen.

Racing

If you use the 'B' for racing you will find it a very forgiving car. Properly set up, it understeers slightly, *i.e.* if you find that you are not quite going to make it round a corner you can put on more lock or, if this fails, a second defence is to simply lift off, which brings the tail round.

The car is so well balanced that you will even get away with braking in corners, which most purists warn against. In any case the 'don't brake in a bend' theory has taken rather a knocking from the Scandinavian rally drivers who are repeatedly braking in corners. Still, this has little application to a paragraph on racing, so let us continue.

All the remarks made about sprints and hill climbs apply to racing, only more so. Power is vital, but if you are a beginner, spend your money first on the suspension and brakes (see page 108), then, when you have experience and confidence, concentrate on getting more power. If you do things the other way round, the car will be faster than you or the roadholding can stand and you may frighten yourself and lose confidence.

During your formative days, keep a log of every circuit you race at, recording which final drive ratio is desirable, the tyre pressures you find best and even random information such as which hotel to stay at in the area, local garages in case you need repairs and so on.

If there are several 'B's in your race have some clearly identifiable mark on yours to help your pit crew and remember that if you are in, say, a ten-lap race with much faster cars competing you may well complete only nine laps before getting the chequered flag.

When you have finished racing for the day, remove your competition numbers unless you propose taking the car home on a trailer.

Rallying

With the joint authors' background, the reader must excuse a bias towards rallies in this particular chapter. They are dealt with after racing, in our financial order, because although the cost of preparing a 'B' for rallying may be no greater than for any other sport, the cost of competing on a long rally can be considerable, with shipping costs, petrol, tyres and hotels.

The type of rally you will encounter will vary according to

which side of the Atlantic you live. In Europe there is very little emphasis on strict timekeeping; the emphasis is more on the ability of the driver to get from A to B quickly and the skill of the co-driver in not getting him lost. There will rarely be any penalty for early arrival, marks are simply lost for being late. Except for international events on which roads are closed for special stages, rallies are largly run at night when the roads are quieter and one gets warning of oncoming traffic by their lights. In North America the events call for much stricter timekeeping and the two types of rally are oceans apart. Americans who have tried the European variety seem to prefer it.

One aspect of the preparation of the car is most important—the electrics. You will want your dip switch readily to foot or hand (some drivers find the standard 'B' dip switch inconvenient and have a steering-column switch instead).

You will also need extra lights mounted on the car; regulations may govern the total number you can fit. Mount additional lights firmly, as a wobbling one can be off-putting on a tight section. Some drivers angle auxiliary lights so that the right-hand one points across to the left and vice versa. Others set one lamp to shine slightly upwards so that they have long-range illumination even when speeding down dips in undulating roads.

Quartz-halogen bulbs are essential for extra lights and they will be used for main lights as dipping bulbs become more freely available. A quartz-halogen bulb gives a higher output than a conventional one from a given wattage by enclosing a tungsten filament in a small quartz envelope; the filament is run at high temperature in gas to which a small quantity of halogen has been added. Sounds complicated, but what it means in practice is very bright lights and once you have used them you won't settle for anything less.

Incidentally, when setting up your lights before the start of a rally do so with the car loaded exactly as it will be on the event. Perspex headlamp covers are marketed for the 'B' which look neat and fair-in the front of the car. Strictly speaking they appear to 'streamline', which is against some regulations, but a scrutineer would have to be splitting hairs to quibble over them.

Tyres are as much a case of driver preference as lights. The works cars always use Dunlops; the SP3 is probably the best general-purpose rally tyre, with Weathermasters for loose or rough going and racers for smooth tarmac (see later chapters). Over recent years there has been an increasing use of racing tyres in rallies and, although they inflict greater stresses on suspension parts, they are certainly quicker.

Depending on the sort of rally you are doing, you may need a twin-speed wiper, demister, efficient heater and, above all, sump and petrol-tank guards (see pages 104 and 105).

Seat belts and a roll-over bar are essential and you and your co-driver may need to add padding here and there (depending on how much natural body fat you have) to protect you from bruising when being thrown about under hard cornering. Use foam rubber and try to make a neat job of it—too often one sees bits of rubber precariously held on here and there with masking tape and so on.

The major item of 'equipment' needed for successful rallying is a co-driver or navigator. The best title is really car manager because this person's job is to look after the office work, leaving you free to devote your undoubted natural talents to driving the car.

On all-night club rallies, the co-driver will be largely occupied with map reading and timekeeping, whereas on a major international he will probably be working from navigation notes which are like the motoring organizations' route instructions ('turn left at cross-roads' and so on), usually prepared by the works teams for their crews but invariably given to private owners as well. 'B' owners are lucky in this respect in that the B.M.C. co-drivers are among the best in the business at making these sort of notes.

With the density of traffic growing all the time, the days of high-speed thrashes across the Continent are over, with the result that most rallies are decided on special stages (Eastern Bloc countries with few cars about and co-operative police are the only places where long fast road sections are still found). Roads are usually closed to other traffic for special stages or else the tests are run on private land (such as in the forests in the U.K.). The marking may involve target times to be beaten but generally the effect is to turn the special stages into flat-out blinds.

The importance of these stages has resulted in the works drivers (as well as the keener private owners) practising over them several times before a rally and making what are known as 'pace notes'. These say 'fast right, then hairpin left, 200 yards then sharp left' and so on and these instructions are called over by the co-driver during the stage. It needs a precise sense of timing and there is no room for ambiguity. To prevent co-drivers losing their voices, through yelling out these instructions, intercom sets are used which consist of microphones mounted on the co-driver's crash hats and speakers put near the driver's ears on their helmets (crash hats are needed on all special stages). The control box for the intercom set can be mounted on the roll-over bar in the 'B'.

Now do you see why the co-driver is so important? It is not an easy job to look down at a set of notes while being driven flat out. The task may be easier if a box is built into the foot well, as short co-drivers find that there is too much leg room in the standard 'B'. As your co-driver puts himself very much in your hands on a rally you should make sure that you are covered against passenger liability.

On most North American events, where timekeeping is more critical than high-speed motoring, the question of staying awake on a rally is not likely to arise, but on European rallies it may pose a problem. If you contemplate using pep tablets to stay awake you *must* consult your doctor first. Many drivers manage without them and some swear by concoctions of fruit juices and so on. Some will tell you that carrot juice is the thing on the basis of the old tale that you never see rabbits wearing glasses—you never see them winning rallies either, though.

One natural hazard you will meet on rallies, but on few other events, is fog and there is little advice one can give on how to cope with it. Some people have the knack of going very rapidly in fog, but this often appears to be due more to bravery than skill. A lot depends on the car—a long bonnet doesn't help in a pea-souper. your co-driver may be able to assist by keeping a close watch on the map and warning you of any sharp turns or junctions, but unless you have a natural talent for fog driving you may find the quickest way through it is to trickle along until someone catches you up, then let them through and follow them.

We could go on for ever—try to avoid doing tests during the half-light at dusk or dawn, scrub-in new tyres before the start of a test, pace yourself on a long rally so that you are fresh for the tough stages and so on. But this didn't set out to be a book on rallying (we don't want to kill the sales of other works available on the subject), so let us conclude this general run-round of the sport with two popular types of competition.

Autocross and Production-car Trials

These are last in our list for convenience, not cost, because if you find you enjoy rallies but are beaten by Scandinavians on loose surfaces, then you might find a season of autocross an advantage. Your car will need a sump guard, good shock absorbers and all-weather tyres, as it probably will for production-car trials. An autocross consists of racing, either in pairs or against the clock, round a field; production-car trials call for you to climb further up hills than the opposition with no time involved. You will be able to take your wife or girl friend with you to bounce up and down on the hills, provided you don't find it too distracting.

Of the events we have covered, you may be able to recoup some of your costs on major races and rallies by way of prize money and trade bonuses (paid by tyre, oil, lighting and other companies to successful users of their products). If you are very successful you may graduate to driving for a works team and you will find this increases your speed because you won't have to worry about going to work in the car the following day.

Even if you don't rise to the height of works driving you can increase your chances of recouping some of your costs by liaising with the works and *not* doing the events they are, but, instead, competing in other events where the opposition will not be so great. The factory may be glad of the chance to widen their publicity coverage and help you with parts for your car or a contribution towards expenses.

There was just one other thing about rallies—don't baulk people; it gets the car a bad name.

CHAPTER 8

PREPARING FOR RALLYING

Preparing an MGB for rallying can cost anything from £5 to £600, depending on just how keen you are to win. Normally, however, a moderate outlay is sufficient to compete in events below international level, and the cost can be cut by doing some of the work in the home garage and by judicious pruning of non-essentials.

Whether one is doing club events in Australia, or preparing for rallying under S.C.C.A. rules in North America; doing the Scottish or Welsh rallies, or entering a big international such as the Monte, it is essential to study the regulations, choose the most suitable class and ensure that modifications carried out on the car will not infringe the regulations.

For rallying in European countries, where most events are run under the International Sporting Code of the Fédération Internationale de l'Automobile (F.I.A.), it is important to study the 'homologation form', obtainable from the R.A.C., 31 Belgrave Square, London, S.W.1.

An homologation form is virtually the birth certificate of a car and lists its dimensions in great detail (together with photographs) to give scrutineers a standard to work from.

When improvements are made to a car or parts are developed which are suitable for competition the factory applies for them to be approved and included on the form. Incidentally, most Canadian rallies are also run under F.I.A. rules.

Anyone new to rallying must obtain a competition licence from the National Club of the respective country in which he or she is resident. The club will also supply any information regarding classes and category that is needed. In the United States, events are run under the rules of the Sports Car Club of America (S.C.C.A.) and cars must not use optional equipment unless it is listed and published by the S.C.C.A.

The MGB is a fairly hardy car and with sound initial preparation a great deal of rallying may be enjoyed without major problems occurring. Even after a few hard club events, however, the car should be checked over if top-line performance is to be retained, *e.g.* brakes may have to be adjusted and drums should be removed and lining dust blown out. Brake shoes and pads, of course, do not last long on bigger events and may need renewal during a long international event even when competition material is used. Decarbonizing, tappet adjustment, adjustment to carburetters and contact points must all be carried out regularly, for although the 'B' has proved its reliability in many gruelling events, like any other piece of machinery it will not tolerate neglect.

A sump guard is essential for rough events such as the R.A.C. and Safari, as well as for many small events which have rough sections. The making and fitting of a guard is something of a trial-and-error job and is dependent upon the facilities available. The best way is to bolt 10 s w g steel across the frame, having it running back far enough to ensure that the front part of the exhaust pipes are protected. Such a guard is by no means lightweight—in fact it just doesn't do the job if it is. Cage nuts welded in the frame prove satisfactory for holding the guard in position, but don't have bolt heads protruding or they will be worn away. They must be countersunk and the bolts should not be less than $\frac{3}{8}$ in. diameter.

Once the guard is in position it will not be a quick job to remove and refit it, so ensure that an oil change is not due.

A hardtop is essential for serious rallying and a crash-roll bar should also be fitted, for both offer a degree of protection if the car is rolled.

Fitting a crash-roll bar involves making brackets and welding. It is not difficult if adequate facilities are available, but the bar should be made of seamless mild-steel tubing of not less than $1\frac{1}{2}$ in. diameter and ·120 in. wall thickness. Don't use chrome-alloy tubing because braces have to be welded to it and apart from the difficulty of welding chrome alloy the strength of the area adjacent to the welds will be impaired if the structure is not normalized.

Use one continual length of tubing for the roll-bar hoop and if it is to be removable make sure that the base of the retaining tubes which the hoop slides into are arc-welded securely to the frame. Gusset plates of 10 s w g will also be needed between the body and tubes. The roll bar must bottom in the tube mountings and two $\frac{3}{8}$ in. diameter bolts each side should be used to retain it. The braces, one each side, should be attached as near to the top of the roll bar as possible and can be bolted at the bottom end to the wheel arch, which should be plated to spread the load.

If a hardtop is fitted, make up brackets from 16 s w g steel to go over the toggle catches to prevent them inadvertently becoming released. Drill a $\frac{5}{16}$ in. clearance hole through the hardtop by each side of the toggle. Secure the brackets with $\frac{5}{16} \times 1$ in. bolts, inserting a flat washer under the heads which should be on the outside of the hardtop. Cover any projections, including the toggles and catches, with foam rubber and wire-lock all bolts as a precautionary measure.

1 & 2 The MGB is seen in competition on such widely differing events as driving tests (above) on smooth tarmac and the old rugged Liège–Sofia–Liège (below). David Hiam and Julian Vernaeve drove number 81 on the 1964 Liège. This was one of the first rally appearances for the model

3 The MGB performs well in long-distance events where reliability is needed. 8 DBL, a well-used works car, was driven to success on the 1965 1000-mile sports car race at Brands Hatch by John Rhodes and Warwick Banks

4 MGB designer Syd Enever modifies the air intake on the 1965 special-bonnet Le Mans car

To avoid hardtop rattles when harder tyre pressures are used, follow the method of tightening suggested on page 133.

As a highly-tuned engine tends to raise the under-bonnet temperature, leading to a decrease in volumetric efficiency, some method of inducing cool air for carburation is advisable. The easiest method is to provide an air intake from the left-hand-side front of the car by means of a length of fresh-air hose. This entails enlarging the hole in the radiator diaphragm to a more suitable size, and fitting a flange (part no. 14B 7712) to hold the trunking in position. The front end of the intake fits close up to the radiator grille and is held by an easily-made clip.

For a quick job, merely enlarging the hole in the diaphragm helps, but it is not quite so effective and tends to reduce unduly the velocity of air through the radiator.

The attachment of trunking direct to the carburetter intake, in an attempt to obtain direct forced ramming, is not really advisable. The fitment of flared pipes to the carburetters when the full race camshaft is used is a much better proposition.

For rallying in hot weather when a hardtop is fitted, or for events such as the Alpine, when the heater may be dispensed with, an added cold-air intake direct to the interior of the car helps crew comfort. To fit the system, once the heater is removed, and the oil-cooler pipes are re-positioned, a suitably-sized hole may be cut in the radiator diaphragm and a flange attached to each side. Run the hose from the diaphragm to the front of the car in the same manner as with carburetter intake. From the rear side of the diaphragm take the trunking to the aperture in the bulkhead where the heater intake normally fits. (This is not normally visible when a heater is fitted.) Another flange of the same type, but with a regulator flap, must be attached to the bulkhead to accept the hose. Parts are listed in the Appendix. (See plate 11.)

Fuel consumption, tanks and protection

The tankage of the latest MGB is 12 Imp. gallons giving, with a standard engine and gearing, a range of approximately 312 miles at 26 to the gallon, under normal driving conditions. Under competition conditions the mileage per gallon, of course, will be worse. While club events can be done on the standard tank, increased tank capacity may be useful on longer events.

From car no. 56743 the car was given a 12 (U.K.) gallon tank in place of the original 10 gallon one and later the old method of retention by means of steel straps was discarded in favour of a flange-type fitment.

Petrol tanks of 23 Imp. gallon capacity are available with the

H

latest flange fitting, but on all cars a section of the trunk floor must be cut out to allow for the extra tank space. Both early and late tourers, however, can be fitted with a supplementary 10 gallon tank in the trunk, although it involves a little cutting and welding to insert the two connecting pipes that are necessary between the two tanks.

If it is decided to go ahead and fit a supplementary tank, the drawings and the parts listed in the Appendix may be obtained from the B.M.C. Special Tuning Department. When the supplementary tank or a larger tank is fitted, the spare wheel is strapped across the tank by means of a retaining strap, part no. AHH 7242.

For most rally and autocross events a protective alloy cover over the base of the petrol tank is advisable. This is comparatively easy to install if the tank is removed and 16 s w g aluminium sheet is shaped to the bottom of the tank. Hold the cover in position with the tank retaining bolts and put a sheet of $\frac{1}{2}$ in. thick foam rubber between the tank and cover. It requires a little patience to get a tight fit but may save damage later.

Dual petrol pumps are advisable and are best fitted in the trunk. The best place in the trunk is close to the offside wheel arch on the floor (see plates 8 and 13).

For all events where the going is likely to be rough it pays to move any vulnerable petrol pipes, brake pipes, battery cables and other electrical wires inside the car.

The standard battery cable and brake pipe are not long enough to re-run inside the car and must be made up according to requirements. Choose the actual position with care so that they will not foul on seat runners, etc. On works cars several different runs have been used with equal success and with commonsense little difficulty should be encountered.

The petrol pipe is best made in two lengths and joined by nuts and a union (see page 192). This helps to avoid kinking when the pipe is placed in position.

When the petrol pumps are mounted in the trunk, some fairly acute bends are necessary, but they can be made without a pipe bender if a little care is exercised. The brake pipe, being of a smaller diameter, is quite easy to manage. When re-piping, take great care to ensure that the pipes run through rubber grommets where they pass through bodywork. Make sure the grommets are a good fit and placed so that they will not be pushed out. The pipes must not chafe; they must not be kinked; they must not be vulnerable to damage and must be firmly clipped in position. A good installation is trouble free. A poor one can be dangerous.

It is also essential when fitting petrol pipes not to place them too near to the exhaust manifold, otherwise vapour lock and percolation troubles can result. In severe cases the former, due to the vaporization of petrol in the fuel line, may result in a complete stoppage, although it more often produces an intermittent fuel supply denoted by bad performance at middle-range speeds. Even hot weather such as is often experienced at the start of the Alpine in the South of France can give rise to vapour lock and produce symptoms of intermittent misfiring when the car is being driven in traffic. Usually percolation is found after a particularly hot fast rally section and occurs when the engine is switched off. It is due to the accumulated heat in the engine compartment causing vapour pressure which forces the petrol regulating needle valve in the float chamber away from its seating; the carburetter then floods and the engine will not start. The combination of a high under-bonnet temperature and badly situated petrol pipes may cause the trouble at low road speeds. Adequate ventilation and a cool location for the pipes is therefore essential.

Map stowage, silencer mountings and mud flaps

Although navigators can often manage without stowage for maps, a leather-cloth bag attached to the navigator's door is a sound idea. An even more important job, however, is to drill all silencer-assembly mounting rubbers and fit bolts to retain the assembly if the rubber bonding breaks away. Use aero-type locknuts on the bolts and do not squash the rubbers when you tighten them.

The standard anchorage points for the safety belts are satisfactory, but the make and type of belt must be a matter of individual preference. Don't attempt to economize here.

For Scandinavia, mud flaps on the front and rear are necessary by law. They have been used on the front during events in other areas, for some drivers feel they help to avoid nails being thrown at the rear tyres, causing punctures.

Brakes

A dual-circuit braking system, such as fitted to the MGB cars sold in America, is advisable for all competitive events where it does not infringe regulations. The fitting of a dual-type system means the use of a special master cylinder and the fitting of new brake pipes.

Needless to say, brakes must always be given top priority, especially if engine performance is increased. Under rally conditions, not only extra lining and pad wear takes place but brake fade may be encountered. The friction material is only a part of the answer and it is essential to ensure that a good competition fluid is used, for it may have to withstand extremely high temperatures.

Anyone familiar with international rallying will have seen front discs glowing cherry red after a special section, and anyone who had to change pads under such circumstances will agree with the advisability of removing the protective stone-guard shields to get extra cooling. Unfortunately competition regulations usually forbid this, but some relief may be obtained by cutting most of the guard off and leaving practically nothing but the retaining brackets. (The regulations allow 'machining and polishing'.) Holes drilled in the guards have been tried with some success but for internationals this is not really sufficient.

For the works rally cars, rear brake shoes fitted with Ferodo VG/95 friction material and front pads of DS 11 are now a fairly standard rally specification although they give a slightly harder pedal. When this friction material is used, however, it pays to change the front/rear braking ratio by fitting smaller ($\frac{3}{4}$ in.) rear-wheel brake cylinders (see page 131), for although the weight transference when braking is virtually unaffected by the extra weight of tanks and rally-type suspension, the change of friction material requires higher hydraulic pressures and there is a tendency for the rear wheels to lock with the standard wheel cylinders.

A servo (kit no. 8G 8732) will reduce the extra pedal pressure necessary when competition linings and pads are used.

The handbrake can be converted to a quick-release 'fly off' type by the fitting of a handbrake pawl and rod, the part numbers are C–AHH 7222 and C–AHH 7223 respectively.

Suspension, tyres and wheels

Although the suspension, steering and tyres are basically separate parts of the car they are nevertheless interrelated in their actions and how they function in relation to each other is extremely important. The specification suggested here is not necessarily the ultimate for any specific job but is for meeting most of the conditions of fast rally driving.

The best specification without unduly changing roll centres or the centre of gravity is achieved by fitting the stronger front coil springs part no. AHH 5789 with the standard $\frac{5}{8}$ anti-roll bar part no. AHH 5793 in conjunction with the police-type rear springs part no. AHH 7346.

For rallies where high speeds over rough going may be necessary the rear rubber spring mountings may be discarded and the springs mounted solidly, using stronger spring centre bolts (see page 128). This type of suspension was fitted to the MGB that went round the punishing Nurburgring for 84 hours to win the Marathon de la Route with Andrew Hedges and Julian Vernaeve.

The GT, as supplied from the factory, is fitted with front springs part no. AHH 5789 and has slightly stronger rear springs than the standard tourer.

The front and rear dampers fitted to the MGB are manufactured by Messrs Armstrong, the front being of the 'top hat' type that were developed for Austin Healey 3000 competition work, the raised body chamber relieving aeration troubles under extreme cornering conditions.

With the stiffer suspension, change the dampers to units with a competition setting. If the existing dampers are in good condition, only the valve assemblies need be changed (see Appendix), but otherwise fit the front competition dampers part no. C–AHH 7104 and the rear dampers part no. C–AHH 7105 for the right hand, and part no. C–AHH 7106 for the left-hand side.

The movement of the suspension produces load changes which affect the tyre forces; these in turn affect stability and as tyres are so important in determining the motional direction of a motor car, careful thought must be given to their choice. First of all, it is advisable to ensure that the correct wheels are fitted.

The standard disc wheels on the tourer are 4 J × 14 and the wire wheels $4\frac{1}{2}$ J × 14, but for most competitive events it is advisable to use wire wheels. The standard $4\frac{1}{2}$ J × 14 wheels are suitable for most club events, but for more serious competition work either $5\frac{1}{2}$ J × 14 Mini-lite magnesium-alloy wheels or $5\frac{1}{2}$ J × 14 wire spoked wheels, which accept a wider-section tyre, are advisable, as they give better adhesion to the road.

To change from disc to wire wheels, the complete rear-axle casing assembly must be changed, for the casing and axle shafts are slightly different, but there is little difficulty (apart from the cost!) in actually making the change-over.

Returning to the matter of tyres: for fast international events on good roads such as the Geneva rally, Alpine, etc., the works rally cars would probably use Dunlop white spot R7 racing tyres which have a tread of great stability and good wet characteristics. The 165×14 radial-ply SP3 on the $5\frac{1}{2}$ J 60 spoke wheels, however, give a wide section and are a good general-purpose tyre for most events. For forest stages the SP 44 Weathermaster is better, while for rallies on ice and snow the SP 44 Weathermaster fitted with studs is ideal.

Any change in tyres affects the calibration of the speedo and Halda Twinmaster, or Speed Pilot, and if this is not remedied at least the co-driver should be aware of the percentage error.

Have all wheel and tyre assemblies dynamically, as well as statically, balanced.

The electrical system

Electrics are extremely important in any rally, and on winter events, where lights and heaters are used for long periods, they prove vulnerable unless properly prepared.

More and more manufacturers are fitting alternators and G–HN4 and G–HD4 cars are fitted with a 16 AC alternator as standard equipment. An alternator can be fitted to older models if desired (see page 132) but a dynamo is quite adequate for most events, apart perhaps from the Monte, when the Lucas 28 amp output dynamo no. 22746 with a matched control box no. 37342 is adequate.

Heavy-duty batteries are available and fit into the standard battery carriers. If an alternator is fitted the heavy-duty batteries are certainly not necessary, but if all the lights are being used and the car is doing a Monte and using a 28 amp output dynamo, then a sound argument might be made for the heavier-duty batteries despite their extra weight.

Headlights with sealed-beam units are not advisable for rallying, for if holed they fail. Conventional headlights with bulbs are much better.

All additional electrical equipment must be fused, Lucas four-way fuse boxes no. 37420 being easiest to fit. Where they are mounted depends a great deal on how much extra equipment is added and how much re-wiring is to be carried out.

Don't forget that the navigator's clocks need to be illuminated, as does any holder for route instructions.

If a compressor-type air horn is used, fuse it separately. The same applies to a two-speed-wiper motor which fits on to the standard brackets and is quite easy to mount, requiring only one extra wire from the switch, which, of course, will require changing to a two-position type.

Fit a competition coil but remount it in a more accessible position; do not fit brand-new contact points to the distributor just before an event; they are best run a few hundred miles first to bed in the contact heel. Trouble from this unit during the event is then unlikely.

A two-pin socket should be mounted on the instrument panel to serve for razors, inspection lights and possibly illuminated map magnifiers. A navigator's horn button is worthwhile and may either be let flush into the floor of the footwell or mounted on a wooden block.

An electric screen-washer model is an asset, but when fitting one include a non-return valve in the system, and fit the switch in a position where it can be operated by the navigator as well as driver.

Waterproof the ignition components with silicone grease, or

use a damp-proof lacquer spray, and place rubber covers over the coil and distributor cap.

The standard starter motor cannot be removed from the car without first removing the oil-filter bottle, and it is advisable to replace it with the smaller competition starter no. 25081 which is easier to change in the event of trouble.

If the rear overriders are removed, a number-plate illumination lamp will be required.

For winter, demister bars are useful.

Close-ratio gears

With a high-output engine, many rally men prefer a close-ratio gearbox for some events. It is inadvisable, however, to change to such gearing haphazardly, just because the car is to be rallied.

When considering close-ratio gears it must be remembered that on the standard first-type gearbox, overdrive can provide useful extra gearing between third and top, but on the close-ratio box the ·802 overdrive when used on third gear is so near to normal top, the ratio being 1·016:1, that it is virtually useless as an intermediate gear though in certain circumstances it can be useful in place of top gear for the sake of the rapid changes it makes possible. On the other hand, overdrive top is a useful extra gear for a highly tuned engine with a close-ratio gearbox, especially when a low axle ratio is used, and allows higher speeds to be maintained for long periods with a minimum of rev/min and less engine stress.

If the overdrive is to be treated as added gearing for arduous competition work, it should be modified by Laycocks' Competitions Department. The modified unit, normally used without the vacuum switch, will give a much more abrupt change so that it should be used in conjunction with the clutch to ease the change and save unnecessary strain on the transmission. On special sections, however, some drivers will decide that the slightly faster changes obtainable may justify the use of the hand switch alone.

While the type of rally may dictate gearbox and final-drive ratios, the permutations of engine tune available are numerous. For most rallying, a moderately-tuned engine as acceptable under F.I.A. Appendix J regulations, with a close-ratio box or, alternatively, with a standard gearbox and 4·55:1 final drive, is a sound all-round specification.

If a change to close-ratio gears is considered, Table 2 gives a comparison with the standard gearbox ratios and also shows the overall ratios with different final drives.

By reference to pages 72–83 it will be found relatively easy to fit the close-ratio gears.

Gearbox Ratio (first-type gearbox)		
	C/R Gears	*Std. Gears*
Top	1·0 : 1	1·0 : 1
Third	1·268 : 1	1·3736 : 1
Second	1·620 : 1	2·2143 : 1
First	2·450 : 1	3·6363 : 1
Reverse	4·7552 : 1	4·7552 : 1

Overall Ratios (Std) 3·909–1 Final Drive		
	C/R Gears	*Std. Gears*
Overdrive (·802)	3·135 : 1	3·135 : 1
Top	3·909 : 1	3·909 : 1
Third O/drive	3·974 : 1	4·306 : 1
Third	4·956 : 1	5·369 : 1
Second	6·332 : 1	8·65 : 1
First	9·577 : 1	14·20 : 1

4·55–1 Final Drive		
Overdrive (·802)	3·649 : 1	3·649 : 1
Top	4·55 : 1	4·55 : 1
Third O/drive	4·627 : 1	5·00 : 1
Third	5·769 : 1	6·24 : 1
Second	7·371 : 1	9·98 : 1
First	11·147 : 1	16·54 : 1

4·3–1 Final Drive		
Overdrive (·802)	3·449 : 1	3·449 : 1
Top	4·30 : 1	4·3 : 1
Third O/drive	4·372 : 1	4·732 : 1
Third	5·452 : 1	5·9 : 1
Second	6·966 : 1	9·52 : 1
First	10·535 : 1	15·63 : 1

4·1–1 Final Drive		
Overdrive (·802)	3·288 : 1	3·288 : 1
Top	4·10 : 1	4·1 : 1
Third O/drive	4·169 : 1	4·515 : 1
Third	5·198 : 1	5·63 : 1
Second	6.642 : 1	9·07 : 1
First	10·045 : 1	14·90 : 1

Standard Gearbox Ratio (second-type gearbox)		
Top	1·0 : 1	
Third	1·382 : 1	
Second	2·167 : 1	
First	3·44 : 1	

The standard ratio on the 'tubed' semi-floating-type axle is 3·909 : 1. A 4·22 : 1, a 4·55 : 1 and a limited slip differential is also available.

TABLE 2

The gears that will be required are 1 first-motion shaft, 1 second-speed gear, 1 third-speed gear and a laygear. The only gears, however, that may be fitted irrespective of any other consideration, as they are suitable for all first-type close-ratio gearboxes, are the third-speed gear C–1H 3300 (29 teeth) and the second-speed gear C–22H 1094 (32 teeth) which must be used with the correct baulk ring 22H 249.

A larger-diameter layshaft (22H 571) than the early standard type is available, but it must be fitted with the caged roller-type bearings 22H 471 and a different distance tube (22H 672) from the standard layshaft, which is part no. 1H 3305.

The part number of the laygear suitable for the large shaft is C–22H 932, while the laygear to fit the small shaft is C–1H 3298.

If the large layshaft is used (and for arduous competitive events it is advisable), it is necessary to have the layshaft mounting holes on the gearbox casing reamed in line to a diameter ·6688 in./·6699 in. (16·98/17·01 mm) or, alternatively, fit new gearbox case assemblies. The casing assembly 48G 314 will be required if overdrive is fitted or, without overdrive, the casing number 48G 315.

On the later first-type gearboxes the first-motion shaft has a larger-diameter spigot and it is important when close-ratio gears are being fitted to take care to fit the correct type. The part numbers are C–22H 472 (26 teeth) for 18G/18GA engines and C–22H 846 (26 teeth) for the 18GB engine.

To convert an early-type gearbox to close ratio and large-type layshaft, the following parts are required (these are, of course, extra to the gaskets and close-ratio gears).

1 Layshaft	22H 571
1 Laygear (close ratio)	C–22H 464
1 Thrust-washer (for laygear, front)	22H 466
1 Thrust-washer (for laygear, rear) ⎤	22H 467
1 Thrust-washer (for laygear, rear) ⎥ alternatives	22H 468
1 Thrust-washer (for laygear, rear) ⎥	22H 469
1 Thrust-washer (for laygear, rear) ⎦	22H 470
4 Caged needle-roller bearings	22H 471
1 Distance piece	22H 672

Should it be decided that the small layshaft will be adequate, the following parts will be required and are equally suitable for 18G/18GA (with the first-motion shaft C–22H 472) and 18GB power units (with first-motion shaft C–22H 846).

1 Laygear	1H 3298	4 Std. circlips	11G 3027
1 Std. layshaft	1H 3305	1 Std. distance tube	11G 3026
3 Std. bearings	3H 2865	Std. thrust-washers as required.	

Building an engine for rallying

Without undue expense it should be possible, with a reasonable degree of mechanical aptitude, to build a sound engine for rally purposes for little more than the cost of the parts. It will be necessary to have a certain amount of machining done, however, particularly on the cylinder head.

The maximum b h p increase possible, consistent with reliability, for rallying the MGB and using readily available parts is about 30%. This entails increasing the capacity of the engine to 1843 cc by boring the cylinder block ·040 O/S.

For lesser requirements the standard bore may be retained and club events may be done using a no more demanding specification than the road-tuning one.

The cylinder head

For all competition work the cylinder head should be flowed and polished, preferably with the combustion chamber polished. The benefit of the latter as regards increased b h p is somewhat infinitesimal perhaps, but to some extent it helps to avoid carbon deposits forming. The squish point should also be cut back a little and radiused. There are numerous tuning shops who specialize in this form of work. North American and Canadian owners can get help from their dealers if they are not doing the work themselves, or it may pay to contact B.M.C./Hambro Inc. (see page 193).

The cylinder head must be machined and the combustion chambers balanced so that their volumes are equal and of the appropriate cubic capacity.

When the engine is turned, as each piston reaches t d c, the crown of the piston should be ·020 in.–·025 in. from the top of its respective bore. In cases where this measurement is excessive the face of the block must either be machined to set this right or allowances made when the cylinder head is machined. Assuming that the cylinder block is correct, an 1843 cc engine with a 39 cc combustion space in the cylinder head and with flat-top pistons has a compression ratio of 10·3:1.

A 1798 cc engine with a head combustion space of 38·7 cc and flat-top pistons will also have a compression ratio of 10·3:1.

An 1821 cc engine (std. + ·020 in.) with a 40 cc head combustion space and flat-top pistons has a compression ratio of 11:1.

These figures are practical examples rather than calculated figures. Slight variations occur with each individual engine due to machining tolerances but their practical effect on the compression ratio is negligible.

If ·009 in. is removed from the cylinder-head face, it reduces the cubic capacity of the head combustion space by 1 cc. It is therefore quite easy to arrive at the correct amount to have removed from the head to obtain any desired compression ratio (see also page 155). The maximum amount removed from the cylinder head by machining, however, must on no account exceed $\frac{3}{32}$ in.

If regulations permit, the valves should be of nimonic alloy, inlet part no. AEH 757 and exhaust AEH 758. Use the bronze (hidural 5) valve guides for both inlet and exhaust valves, pressing them into position so that they are left standing out between $\frac{42}{64}$ and $\frac{25}{32}$ in. from the machined face of the valve-spring seating. Make sure that the valves are seating properly and after lapping them in and giving all the components a thorough clean, assemble the head using outer 130 lb valve springs part no C–AHH 7264, and inner 60 lb valve springs part no. C–AHH 7265. When the nimonic valves are fitted, special valve cotters and top and bottom spring caps must be used, and the standard metal shroud should be discarded and the head assembled without the valve-stem oil seals. This assembly will allow up to 6600 rev/min with the competition camshafts and up to 6400 rev/min with the standard camshaft.

The standard rocker shaft with the strengthened rockers 12H 2037 may be used but it is not advisable to unduly lighten them, for rockers are highly-stressed components. Loading is greatest near the fulcrum, therefore if metal is removed take it off as near each extremity as possible, preferably at the valve-stem end by removing the metal from the sides of the area that contacts the stem of the valve·

Although by no means essential, the rockers may also be polished, for it is easier to inspect them for any flaws and the polishing helps to counteract fatigue failure.

Special rocker-shaft end brackets are available which fit at each end of the shaft to support it from each side of the rocker. They are not acceptable under Appendix J or S.C.C.A. rules, however. The same applies to the steel tubular distance pieces which are obtainable to replace the rocker-shaft springs and although the tubes marginally help reduce frictional losses they tend to increase tappet noise at idling speed. If the distance pieces are used, ensure they have ·003 in. end float when assembled on the engine.

While on the subject of the rocker assembly, it is worth noting that although the standard tappet-adjusting screws are quite strong, they may be replaced with a stronger solid type, the oiling of the push-rod ball-cup being adequate without the lubrication drilling. For rallying, the stronger type are not absolutely essential and are more for long-distance racing or record breaking. When the rockers are assembled, line them up with the valve stem, making any minor adjustments necessary.

Camshafts and timing gear

There are two camshafts available, usually termed half-race and full-race, part numbers C–AEH 714 and C–AEH 770 respectively.

The half-race camshaft gives a ·250 in. cam lift with 268° period for inlet and exhaust. Inlet opens 24° b d t c and closes 64° a b d c. Exhaust opens 59° b b d c and closes 29° a t d c. The tappet setting is ·017 in. when hot.

The full-race high-lift camshaft gives a cam lift of ·315 in, and a valve lift of ·452 in. The inlet period and the exhaust period is 300°. Inlet opens 50° b t d c and closes 70° a b d c. Exhaust opens 75° b b d c and closes 45° a t d c. The tappet setting when hot is ·018. For most rallies, the full-race-type camshaft is advisable, although for minor events the half-race is somewhat smoother in performance with slightly-better torque characteristics. When the high-lift camshaft is used, the face of the cylinder block must be recessed to allow the exhaust valves full travel.

With the extra stresses imposed on the timing gear it is also advisable, if regulations permit, to fit the steel crankshaft sprocket and camshaft timing-chain sprocket. It is also possible to fit larger dimension cam-followers to the 'B' engine, but for rallying they are not essential (see Tuning for racing).

Cylinder block and pistons

When fitting a high-lift camshaft, the cylinder block must be machined to allow the valves full travel. To do this it is necessary to obtain a flat cutter $1\frac{7}{32}$ in. diameter preferably with a $\frac{1}{16}$ in. radius on the outer cutting corner.

The machining must be done from the valve guide centre and the recesses cut approximately $\frac{9}{64}$ in. deep. On final assembly, after tappet adjustment is carried out, check that when the exhaust valves are in their fully open position there is a minimum clearance of ·050 in. between the fully open exhaust valve and recessed cylinder-block face.

If difficulty is encountered in obtaining a cutter, the job may be given to a machine shop, or a cutter as shown in fig. 8: 1 may be used. This is made by brazing small pieces of tool steel to an old valve and grinding them to shape as shown in the diagram. In operation, it is placed in the appropriate position in the cylinder head which is then fitted to the block and held down with a couple of nuts. The block is stood on the table of a bench drill and the top of the valve stem gripped tightly in the drill chuck. The drill should be run at low speed and the cutter advanced very slowly downwards with the drill feed lever.

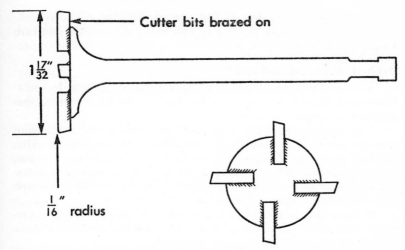

Cutter bits brazed on

$1\frac{17}{32}''$

$\frac{1}{16}''$ radius

Fig. 8:1 Cutting tool for recessing cylinder block, made up from an old valve

When cutting the recesses, do not make them deeper than necessary, and make doubly sure to check the clearance when the exhaust valve is fully open. If the engine capacity is to be increased to 1843 this necessitates having the cylinders bored and using + ·040 in. grade 1 or grade 2 flat-top high-compression pistons part no. AEH 685143, which are fitted with fully-floating gudgeon pins.

On the 18G/18GA engine, if a standard 1798 cc engine is being built, the competition standard-sized flat-top pistons part no. C–AEH 736 with fully floating gudgeon pins may be fitted. The use of these pistons means fitting the bushed con-rods part no. AEH 642 for cylinders 2 and 4 and part no. AEH 644 for cylinders 1 and 3.

If the cylinder block needs reboring, + ·020 in. oversize pistons with fully-floating gudgeon pins for use with the bushed rods are also available (see page 189).

It should be noted that the high-compression pistons have a working clearance of ·007 in. which is allowed for in the piston manufacture. If reboring is carried out, the normal bore size plus the oversize gives the correct-sized bore.

Before the cylinder-head retaining studs are replaced in the cylinder block, lightly countersink the stud holes. This avoids the metal around the holes pulling up, so ensuring a better seal when the head is bolted down. It also pays to use extra-thick flat washers under the cylinder-head nuts; ideally they want turning from 40 ton steel and should be $\frac{3}{32}$ in. thick with a $\frac{3}{4}$ in. outside diameter and a ·390 in. diameter hole.

It is important to ensure that the competition cylinder-head gasket part no. C–AEH 768 is used and to lap the cylinder head to the block face.

Flywheel, crankshaft and clutch

The standard crankshaft on the 18G/18GA engine is quite robust and suitable for minor rallies, but it must be used with the standard bearings.

The special crankshaft fitted with the racing clearance main bearings and big-end bearings is advisable for all hard events. The standard cast-iron flywheel is amenable to lightening but the lightening should not be overdone, for with the considerable gear-changing necessary during a rally the consequent heat transference from the clutch will not be adequately absorbed.

If lightening is carried out, it is essential to drill and peg the starter ring-gear to the flywheel and to have the crankshaft, flywheel and clutch assembly dynamically balanced.

The competition clutch is essential, for it has a stronger diaphragm spring and a driven plate that is bonded as well as riveted. The clutch pit ideally requires a little added ventilation, but here you not only have to watch regulations but guard against the danger of stones getting into the clutch housing. If a sump guard is used this solves the latter problem. Full details of the added ventilation will be found in Chapter 9.

Lubrication system

On all engines used for competitive purposes, it is advisable to machine the oil-pump cover to prevent the tendency of the oil pressure to drop off at high revolutions. The machining operation required on the three-main-bearing 18G/18GA engine oil pump is depicted in fig. 3:9 and is different to the rather simpler machining on the 18GB pump which can be seen by reference to plate 6.

When reassembling the oil pump on early engines check the threaded attachment plate on the oil strainer where it is spot welded to the inside face of the strainer top plate. Make sure that the top plate is flat and that the attachment plate has pulled up correctly to the underside of the top plate when spot welded, for an air leak at this point can produce a momentary lack of oil pressure under certain conditions of oil surge if the level is low. When reassembling the unit, ensure that the top plate is flat over the gasket area and be sure to fit a new gasket. On competition engines it is advisable to increase the oil flow from the filter by carrying out the machining operation in fig. 8:2. To do this it is necessary to remove the circular plate from the filter body. After the machining has been carried out,

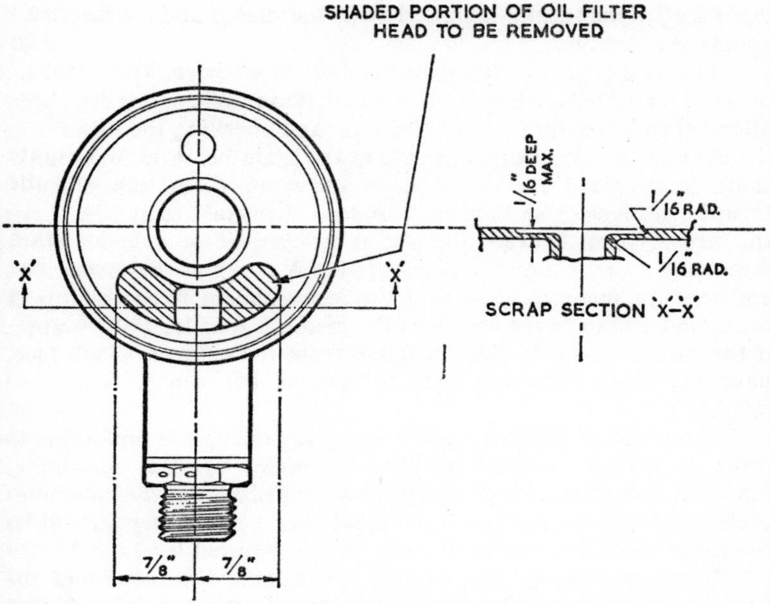

SHADED PORTION OF OIL FILTER
HEAD TO BE REMOVED

Fig. 8:2. Diagram showing portion of oil filter head to be removed. The machining indicated allows a better oil flow and is advisable if the car is to be used for high-speed competitive events

refit the plate and ensure that it remains in position by carefully peening a little of the filter body over the plate.

When the extra-clearance bearings are used, it is necessary to increase the oil pressure. Packing pieces may be inserted behind the oil-release-valve spring to achieve this. It is best to obtain, or make up, two pieces ·100 in. thick and $\frac{3}{4}$ in diameter. In this way any subsequent adjustment can easily be made after the engine has been running and the pressure noted.

Pre-assembly of crankshaft and pistons

If a competition engine is being built, for rallying or for racing, some notes on procedure may help. (General assembly is given in Chapter 4.) If the basic unit is built entirely from new parts this avoids having the car off the road for a time. It does involve added expenditure, of course, but it is worth considering, for the engine modifications cannot be carried out very quickly unless considerable equipment happens to be at hand.

When all the necessary parts have been obtained, have the cylinder head polished and the flywheel lightened. Then have the crankshaft dynamically balanced with the clutch and flywheel as a complete assembly.

The next step is to have the cylinder block bored to + ·040 in. oversize or whatever has been decided upon. When this has been attended to, after thoroughly cleaning, and checking the oilways in the cylinder block and crankshaft, fit the main bearings and crankshaft. Install no. 1 and no. 4 piston and con-rod and subsequently turn the crankshaft so that no. 1 and no. 4 piston are at t d c. Take the measurement between the piston crown and the cylinder-block face using a dial gauge. The cylinder block may now be dismantled and sent for machining, so that the measurement from the top of the cylinder bore to the crown of the piston is ·025 in. For instance, if the piston crown is ·030 in. down from the cylinder block face, have the block face machined to remove between ·005 in. and ·010 in.

If a polished cylinder head is being obtained, it is preferable to order it with the correct combustion space volume. Assuming, however, that the existing head has been polished and the volume of each combustion space has been equalized, the next step should be to reduce the volume of each space to the required level.

If a compression ratio of 10·5:1 is desired the volume of the head space must be 39 cc (see page 155). If the capacity of each cylinder-head combustion space is 42·5 cc this entails machining the head face to reduce the volume of the combustion space by 3·5 cc.

As the removal of ·009 in. from the cylinder-head face reduces the head combustion space by approximately 1 cc, in order to reduce the volume by $3\frac{1}{2}$ cc, ·0315 (·009 × 3·5) must be machined from the head face to give a c r of 10·5:1.

To work out a c r of 11:1 for an 1843 cc engine with flat-top pistons: by turning to the Appendix we find that the unswept volume of the cylinder bore is 4·08 cc and that the volume of the combustion space due to the thickness of the cylinder-head gasket (compressed) is 4·86 cc. We also find that the volume of the cylinder-head space needs to be 37 cc and that the volume of one cylinder is 460·75 cc.

$$c\,r = \frac{\text{Volume of cylinder plus volume of combustion space}}{\text{Volume of combustion space}}$$

$$\therefore \quad \frac{460\cdot75 + 37 + 4\cdot08 + 4\cdot86}{37 + 4\cdot08 + 4\cdot86} = c\,r$$

$$\therefore \quad \frac{506\cdot69}{45\cdot94} = 11{:}1 \; c\,r$$

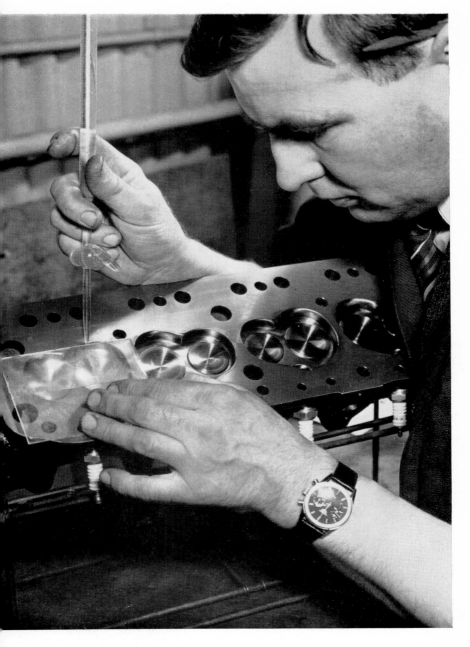

5 Co-author John Organ checking the capacity of combustion spaces on an MGB cylinder head

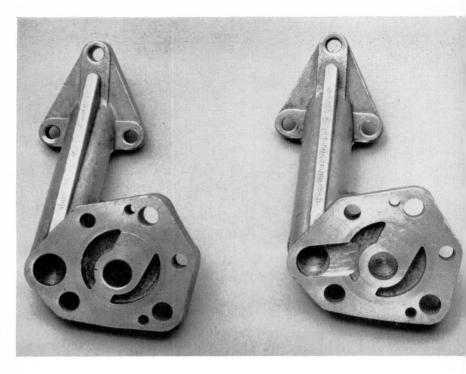

6 Comparison of the two oil pump covers shows (right) the machining of the oilway to increase oil flow at high speed, only necessary if high rev/min are to be sustained for long periods

7 The Tecalemit Jackson fuel-injection system fitted to an MGB engine

8 A GT fitted with a 20-gallon fuel tank and large filter neck

9 Bumpers off and an external bonnet pull (near the left headlamp)—
but watch the regulations over points like these

10 Ducting, to reduce the under-bonnet temperature, is easily fitted

11 A method of keeping the driver cool. A direct fresh-air duct
replaces the heater unit

Before assembling the engine, chamfer the cylinder-head stud holes (see page 117) and lap the cylinder head and cylinder-block face together, using a fine carborundum paste. Needless to say, it is essential to thoroughly clean all the parts before assembly (see Chapter 4).

Manifolds and carburetters

The lightweight steel exhaust manifold is superior to the standard type and whenever it comes within regulations should certainly be fitted. If, however, the standard type has to be fitted, grind the exhaust manifold ports slightly larger than those in the head so that there cannot be any restriction to gas flow. As the standard manifolds are not a one-piece casting, which would entail all exhaust gases running directly to one pipe after they have left the cylinder head, the manifolds are quite effective although the inter-cylinder interference is nevertheless slightly greater than with the steel tube manifold.

N64Y Champion sparking plugs (or their equivalent) will be needed for compression ratios of 10·5:1. A 40943 Lucas distributor has a suitable advance curve for the full-race camshaft and should be set with a static ignition setting of 6° b t d c. If, however, the half-race shaft is fitted the standard Lucas distributor with static ignition setting of 10° b t d c should be fitted.

Although a twin-choke Weber carburetter, together with inlet manifold and the necessary parts for fitting, is available for the MGB engine, it will not always comply with competition regulations. The gain with the Weber, however, can be as much as 10 b h p at 6000 rev/min, over the 1¾ in. twin SU carburetters, with better acceleration.

The 1¾ in. HS6 SU carburetters are four-bolt fixing but fit on to the standard inlet manifold without difficulty, although it is only possible to retain each carburetter with two retaining studs and nuts. With the standard manifold, the heat shield can be retained, but line the system up with the gaskets and heat insulating blocks on the bench before finally assembling the cylinder head.

An inlet manifold with four-bolt carburetter retention flanges is also available but it is not homologated at the time of writing.

Some special points to watch are to wire-lock the banjo bolts, and to ensure that the carburetter overflow pipes are not blocked by foreign matter or kinking. The standard fan should be fitted and the inlet manifold lined up to the cylinder-head ports.

MGBs can be made to go even faster with supercharging equipment, Weber carburetters or an HRG head with fuel injection (see page 122), but the regulations of the bigger events so penalize their use that they are seldom advisable.

I

CHAPTER 9

TUNING FOR RACING

Whether tuning for a single long race or for a season's club racing the aim is obviously going to be the same, *i.e.* good braking and road holding with as much power as possible, commensurate with reliability and your purse.

On the track, money spent on the car does not necessarily mean success, it must be combined with skill and know-how; the latter often learned by comparisons of lap times, modifications and alterations, thought and enthusiasm. The newcomer should make haste slowly and develop his own driving before spending too much on his car. Concentrate on road holding first, obtaining power later if you feel you have the talent. Rather than suggest any definite engine specification for racing, the basic essentials are given with an indication of what is available; it should therefore be possible to develop a racer according to one's progress and pocket.

Ideally, if as much power as possible is going to be squeezed from an MGB, the cylinder block should be bored to ·040 in. oversize to increase the cubic capacity to 1843 cc (as suggested in the previous chapter).

Basically, the engine specification may consist of the standard B.M.C. stage 6 tune, either with SU carburetters or, for more power, with a single 45 DCOE 13 Weber twin-choke carburetter. This specification, when used with the steel exhaust manifold, can be relied upon for 130 b h p with a standard bore, or slightly more with a ·040 in. oversize bore.

The Downton head, of an appropriate compression ratio, may be used with the hidural valve guides and nimonic valves and the strong valve springs, part number (outer) C–AHH 7264, (inner) C–AHH 7265. Siamese ported heads, however, seldom produce the power of a well-designed head that has separate ports for each cylinder and the HRG Mark III alloy cylinder head (available from Derrington Engineering), with larger valves, is well worth considering. Compression ratios of up to 12:1 can be obtained by the use of special pistons, though normally a compression ratio well below this is advisable and will give plenty of extra power.

Fuel injection

The HRG cylinder head may be used with two twin-choke

POWER CURVES OF 18 GB ENGINE
STANDARD AND TUNED TO STAGE 6

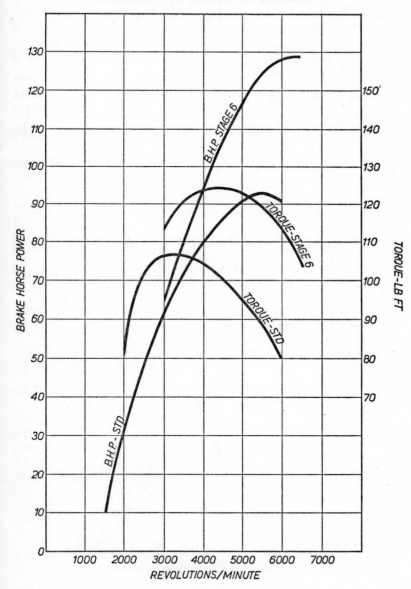

Fig. 9:1

Weber carburetters or with the Tecalamit-Jackson fuel-injection
system, which can also be supplied by Derringtons, when it will
increase the bhp by approximately 10%. The system is of the con-
tinuous injection type and can be used for normal road work if
desired but can only be fitted to an engine that has individual intake
ports for each cylinder. It is therefore only suitable for the MGB
when a four-inlet-port cylinder head is used.

Avoiding fatigue failures

On a racing engine, the possibility of fatigue cracks and the
consequent failure of engine components due to repeated vibration-
ary loading and fluctuating stresses may be relieved by careful
attention to the metal surface condition of components. Fatigue and
stress cracks invariably occur at the surface and progress inwards
until complete fracture occurs. Usually, fatigue develops at some
concentration of stress, often where there is a change of section or
diameter, or at a keyway, or a sharp edge, or on a poorly-radiused
area.

Although all new engine and gearbox components to be used
for racing should ideally be crack tested, this is not the complete
answer, for though it may detect cracks which have occurred during
manufacture, fatigue cracks occur after components are in service.
Moreover, fatigue cracks in their early stage are invariably extremely
fine and it is difficult to detect a new fatigue crack that is less than
$\frac{3}{16}$ in. in length, unless its presence is actually suspected. However,
in spite of the difficulties, the use of inexpensive crack-detecting kits,
of both the magnetic and dye-penetrant types, are well worth while
when a racing engine is stripped for overhaul. In the USA the
Magnaflux Corporation, which was one of the pioneers of non-
destructive metal testing involving the principles of magnetic particle
inspection, is thought of very highly. In North America many dye-
penetrant kits are also available, *e.g.* the Dubl-Check and Flaw-
Finder.

Apart from detecting cracks, the object should be of course to
avoid them. The careful removal of stress-raising surface irregulari-
ties and stress concentration points by polishing, while a tedious
job, is nevertheless the correct approach. The 'B' series engine is of
a robust construction and if B.M.C. Competition parts are used
there is little reason to expect trouble; stress concentration points to
watch on any engine, however, are rivet holes, especially where fan
blades are drilled and rivetted to central hubs, or where metal is
removed from components, or lightening holes are drilled.

Attention to cam-followers

Some attention to the cam-followers is advisable on the MGB because the short life of these components on pushrod engines is notorious, especially when they have to meet the extra stresses which are imposed by the fitting of a high-lift camshaft. On the 'B' series engine, relief from cam-follower trouble can be achieved to some extent by fitting the larger cam-followers, part no. AEC 264. To do this the cam-follower bores in the cylinder block must be opened up to a diameter of ·9375 in. and enough metal taken out above the cam-follower bores to facilitate placement of the cam-followers. The fitting of the larger cam-followers entails the use of the shorter pushrods, part no. C–AEH 767.

The special rocker end brackets and rocker spacer tubes, together with the stronger rockers part no. 12H 3037, should be regarded as essential, but the rockers may be lightened and polished with advantage (see page 115).

The prevention of oil surge

Whatever basic engine tune is decided upon, when racing an MGB, it is essential to fit a deeper, higher-capacity sump with an oil baffle and to lengthen the oil pick-up. This ensures a sufficient head of oil above the strainer pick-up and prevents surge problems occurring. The oil pump, as well as the sump, on the 18G/18GA engine is different to the GB engines and so requires different packing pieces to extend the pump strainer. For 18G/18GA engines the part numbers for the sump and requisite packing piece for the oil pump are C–AHH 7252 and C–AHH 7238 respectively. For the deep 18GB sump and packing piece the part numbers are C–AEH 832 and C–AEH 847 respectively. A suitable oil baffle for the 18G/18GA engine is depicted in fig. 9:2.

Lightening and balancing

For a racing engine with high revolutions in constant use, lightening and balancing assumes added importance and the extra smoothness and power imparted by a well-balanced flywheel/crank assembly is of course essential. As an example, the change to Brabham balanced assemblies for the 1275 Mini Coopers of the B.M.C. Competition Department undoubtedly played a big part in the extra power obtained in the latter half of 1966 and early 1967.

The balancing, lightening and polishing of the connecting rods is important on any racing engine, and greatly helps acceleration by reducing inertia stresses, and undue loading on the bearings. Even before balancing is contemplated, however, the con-rod length

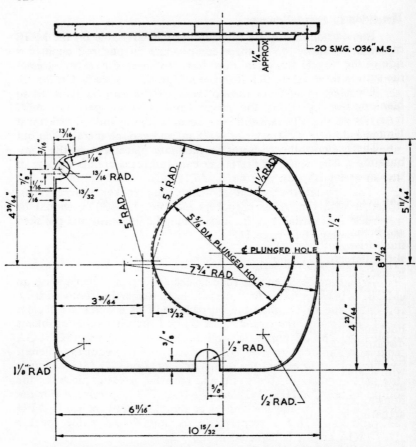

Fig. 9:2. An oil sump baffle plate is essential for racing. The measurements apply to 18G/18GA engines

between centres should be checked, for production tolerances of any volume-produced car are wider than on a car designed and built purely for racing. The equalizing of con-rod weight is easy enough, but to obtain an equal balance of weight on all rods in all 'planes' is by no means easy, and entails the use of especially-adapted equipment and needs time and patience.

The full potential of the 'B' series engine modifications would probably be more fully realized by fitting a free-rolling crank on roller bearings—a task for only the most dedicated designer and tuner!

The cooling system

The design of the MGB water-pump impeller is such that cavitation, which in effect is the formation of steam on the suction side of the pump, does not occur within the rev range possible, and the standard water-pump pulley may be used.

The engine should be run without the thermostat, but a by-pass blanking insert must be fitted in its place. Under some conditions it may be beneficial to dispense with the fan, but for club racing in the United Kingdom a standard three-bladed one is usually advisable.

The heater, of course, will be dispensed with and air for carburation purposes obtained by running an air hose to the front of the car as for rallying (see page 133).

The gear ratio and the clutch

Close-ratio gears are essential for all racing and the first-type gearboxes must be fitted with the larger layshaft (see page 113). The final-drive ratio depends a great deal upon the circuit, but a limited slip differential available from B.M.C. Special Tuning Department is also valuable.

The special competition clutch must be used, and the clutch housing should be modified by cutting a $\frac{5}{8}$ in. diameter hole to replace the small hole and split pin in the bottom wall of the clutch bell housing. The rubber bellows over the clutch actuating lever must be discarded and a hole at the top centre of the bell housing and 3 in. down from the bolting flange is also required. This must be covered with a square metal box 2 in. × 2 in. × $\frac{5}{8}$ in. with a $\frac{3}{8}$ in. fixing flange and must be open at one side. The box should be riveted to the bell housing and arranged so that the open side faces towards the clutch-actuating lever side of the gearbox.

Everything possible must be done to reduce weight (lightweight seats, etc.) and all bolts should be wirelocked when possible. An engine steady bracket should be arranged and fits quite neatly on to the rear engine-bearer plate.

Open-cockpit racing

An open cockpit with a standard windscreen completely alters the air-flow pattern over a sports car; the MGB tourer is no exception and maximum speed is always obtained with a hardtop, or with the hood erected and side windows up. A tonneau cover over the passenger seat, however, and just a single small aero screen for the driver, with spats fitted over the rear wheel openings, can reduce the drag co-efficient by 8–10% and reduces the frontal area by nearly 20% and is therefore the ideal.

Covers over the rear-wheel openings, however, are impossible for almost everything except record breaking (or short races where wheel removal will not be necessary).

Open racers in North America are the rule rather than the exception, for all S.C.C.A. racing—and that covers the greatest proportion by far of sports-car racing—is 'open cockpit' because S.C.C.A. regulations do not permit the use of an attached hardtop or fabric top even if those items are part of the original equipment.

The suspension

For racing the best suspension specification entails the use of the Sebring front springs EX 235/9 and the rear springs, part no. AHH 7346, lowered 1 in. by reducing the camber.

For long events, with constant gear changing and acceleration throwing extra work on the rear springs and spring centre bolts, the rubber spring mountings may be discarded and stronger centre bolts fitted. This necessitates the removal of the axle and the springs from the car. When this has been attended to, each spring centre bolt must be replaced by an Allen bolt 3 in. long and $\frac{5}{16}$ in. diameter with a $\frac{7}{16}$ in. head. The locating holes in the axle, which accept the rubber mounting and centre bolt, must now be modified by welding-in a suitable-sized ferrule to accept the new spring centre bolt. With this done the fitting surface must be refaced.

On assembling the springs to the axle casing, insert a fibre pad $\frac{1}{16}$ in. thick between the spring and case. The 'U' bolts for the 'police' springs, part no. AAA 3838, must be used but may need the removal of a few threads. Check that the nuts do not come to the end of the thread when they are tightened.

If the spring rubber-mounting is retained, standard production 'U' bolts may be used, although they must be checked for length.

If Dunlop R7 tyres are used, ensure that they have clearance, for it is nearly always necessary to do a little doctoring around the inside and outer side of the wheel arch. Obvious fouling points such as protruding self-tapping screws or bolts and nuts that may have been added must also be carefully watched. It is also necessary to remove the rear shock-absorber retaining bolts and to reduce the bolt-head thickness by 50%.

For the front, an anti-roll bar is essential, so too are shock absorbers with a competition setting.

The braking system

The rear brake-shoe friction material should be Ferodo VG 95 or similar, for these linings are of a moulded material with a brass wire core and have exceptionally long life under arduous conditions. Moreover VG 95s have a 165°C higher operating temperature than standard AM 12 Ferodo material. The DS 11 pads should be used on the front brakes for they have excellent resistance to fade (see fig. 9:3) with a low wear rate. The friction material is of a rigid moulded form, dark grey in colour. It has a metallic inclusion in the form of copper particles and is a pad widely used for rallying as well as racing and has a maximum operating temperature of 900°C (disc temperature) against the MGB Ferodo pad maximum (material DA 6) of 600°C.

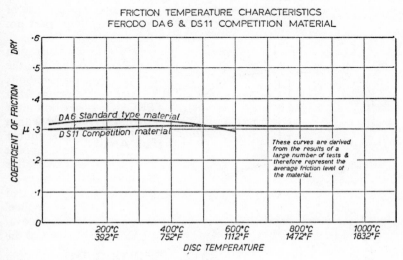

FRICTION TEMPERATURE CHARACTERISTICS
FERODO DA 6 & DS 11 COMPETITION MATERIAL

Fig. 9:3

For short events the standard-sized DS 11 pads can be fitted, but DS 11 pads with a larger friction area are available (see fig. 9:4) and should be used for all very long races. While the larger pads do not improve braking (indeed at a given line pressure, as the contact area is larger, the braking would be slightly less) they do have a considerably longer life and were used at Nurburgring in the 1966 Marathon de la Route, the winning car needing only one pad change. The pads, like the smaller-area types, have a deep cut dividing the material almost into two separate entities. All MGB pads for racing are now supplied in this form which evolved from development work by Ferodo on Formula 1 Grand Prix cars to avoid pad curl, due to the heat intensity at the centre of the pad facing. The dividing of the pad into virtually two separate facings is said to reduce the heat in the centre of the pad by forming two heat centres on what is still virtually one pad.

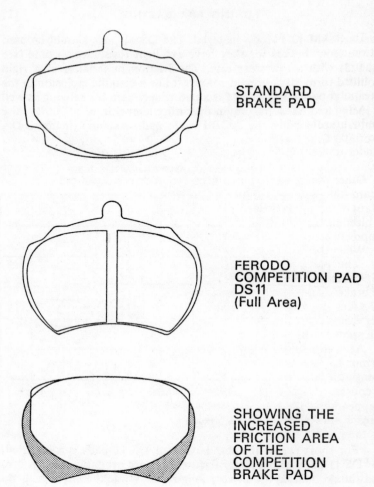

STANDARD BRAKE PAD

FERODO COMPETITION PAD DS 11 (Full Area)

SHOWING THE INCREASED FRICTION AREA OF THE COMPETITION BRAKE PAD

Colour coding of brake pads.

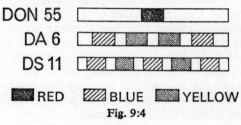

DON 55

DA 6

DS 11

RED   BLUE   YELLOW

Fig. 9:4

To obtain a more satisfactory braking ratio when the different friction material is used, smaller wheel-cylinders ($\frac{3}{4}$ in.) must be fitted to the rear brakes. As the wheel-cylinders have a locating dowel on the fitting face, the brake back plate will have to be drilled to correspond with that of the new cylinder.

After removal of the existing wheel-cylinder, fill the unrequired hole by brazing a small stud into position and face off. Drill the new hole ·170 in. to ·175 in. so that it is ·578 in. above the centre of the cylinder-mounting hole and ·350 in. offset from the radial centre line.

Other points to watch when fitting the new brake shoes are to discard the shoe steady springs, pins and washers, and to make certain to get all of the air from the system. While this may be done by bleeding in the usual manner (see page 67), pressure-bleeding equipment is recommended and invariably results in a firmer pedal.

When the car is first taken on the road, bed the brakes in gradually. The pads will be satisfactory after a few applications but VG/95 linings take a considerable time. The quickest way is to have the brake drums sand blasted, although even when this is done, it still takes quite a time. Another method is to remove the drums after every dozen or so applications of the brakes and remove the high spots from the linings with a coarse file.

As soon as the brakes are bedded, they must be faded. Do not attempt to fade them before they are bedded otherwise the brake drums may be ruined, due to local hot spots. Fading is accomplished by constant hard applications of the pedal until all braking effect disappears. A little help may be given by light handbrake application to reach this stage more quickly. On subsequent recovery (it takes less than half a minute) the brakes may be used hard without fade.

Oil cooler, plugs and battery

For racing purposes the larger competition oil cooler should be fitted. N62R Champion sparking plugs or the cooler grade N57R are suitable, but much depends on the final specification.

When regulations permit, a small race-type 12 volt battery may replace the two standard 6 volt batteries and will help reduce weight.

One final point. A newcomer to racing should fit the largest rear-view mirror he can find—and use it.

CHAPTER 10

OPTIONAL EXTRAS AND ACCESSORIES

While there are a number of 'factory' optional extras available for the MGB and quite a few accessories which are factory approved, there are also numerous items manufactured by companies other than B.M.C. that may be of interest.

'Optionals' are best fitted when the car is built (they may be cheaper this way) but approved accessories which have been examined, tested and often developed in conjunction with the MG design department are usually fitted independently of the factory.

Although twin horns are an optional extra on export cars, these horns can also be purchased through B.M.C. Service. The Fiam compressor type produces a more penetrating note, but for competition work, where weight is also a consideration, Mixo-minor are small and practically as good.

Few motorists these days purchase a new car without a fresh-air heater but anyone who has bought a second-hand car without a heater and wants to fit one can obtain an installation kit.

There are numerous small items, such as an ashtray for mounting on the gearbox tunnel, a map pocket for fitting to the left-hand side of the passenger foot-well, a demist panel and chrome trim for the exhaust pipe, that all have their uses. Others are a luggage grid, cigarette lighter and a locking petrol filler cap. Fog lamps and long-range driving lamps for fitting to the radiator grille are available from most B.M.C. distributors.

Rear vision on the GT can be improved under certain conditions by fitting a heated rear-window light. If, however, the car has a dynamo installation, is regularly driven short distances, and other auxiliary electrical equipment is fitted, the battery may not get sufficient charge. An alternator will take care of this, for one of the principal advantages of this charging equipment is that a high maximum output is obtained at low speeds.

When fitting an alternator it is important to make certain that the control box is mounted vertically with the terminals facing downwards. Choose a cool position for the box and do not use a smaller cable size than stated on the wiring diagram (see page 166).

There are several important things to remember once the installation has been completed. On no account must the engine be run with the battery disconnected, otherwise the control unit may be damaged. Also, if a fast charger to boost the battery has to be used make certain that the ignition switch remains off at all times, while if a fast charger is ever connected just to get a temporary boost to start the engine the 4 TR control unit must be disconnected.

A sun roof for the GT

Anyone who wants a sunshine roof on their GT will find Tudor Webasto do an excellent conversion and used in conjuction with a wind deflector gives one the advantages of fresh-air motoring without draughts. The installation is neat and unobtrusive and the roof can be slid back and locked in any position. The interior is rendered to match the standard roof trim, while the exterior can be finished in any B.M.C. colour to match the car. (See plate 16.)

In spite of the large size of the sliding roof, a specially prepared seasoned ash frame fitted to the inside of the body and secured by countersunk screws ensures that the torsional strength of the roof is not sacrificed. Added reinforcement of the body structure is carried out by fitting 16 swg steel plates to the door and window-pillar points. Installation, by specially appointed fitting stations, usually takes about a week.

The wind deflector, made from tinted 'Oroglass', cuts down glare and wind noise.

Hardtops

Apart from the standard factory hardtops, several others are available. One interesting variation is the GT type, with hinged quarter-light windows.

Another interesting variation is the 'Bermuda' hardtop by Classic Motor Crafts. Made of laminated glass-fibre plastic with roof lights and rear quarter-lights, it has a slightly concave-curved rear-view panel of $\frac{1}{8}$ in. clear perspex set in rubber beading with 'plastic chrome' insert. (See plates 14 and 15.)

One of the worst things about hardtops is a tendency to rattle, especially when used for rallying or racing, with harder tyre pressures and stiffer suspensions. Most of this trouble on the B.M.C. hardtop can be traced to improper adjustment. The driver's handbook supplied with the car details the way to ensure a good fit, with freedom from rattles, but for anyone who has mislaid the handbook here are the instructions reprinted verbatim: 'Assemble the quarter-panel side brackets to the side sockets on the car, using a spring washer under the head of the bolt. Tighten the single bolt securing each bracket and remove the hardtop securing bolts complete with their four washers; keep these ready to hand.

'With one person at each side, lift the hardtop into position over the rear of the car.

'Lower the rear end of the hardtop and engage the anchor plate brackets with the car anchor plates. Difficulty will be met if the rear sealing rubber is not clear of the anchor-plate brackets.

'Centralize the hardtop to the car by lining up the hardtop drip moulding with the rear-wing top beading.

'Apply hand pressure evenly to the rear of the hardtop and check that the front toggle-fastener tongues are in their sockets on the windscreen with the front sealing rubber forward of the wind-screen top. In this position, with pressure still applied from the rear, insert the quarter-panel side-bracket bolts, one each side, with one washer under the head of the bolt and the other three between the bracket on the hardtop and the bracket on the side socket of the car. *Do not tighten the bolts down fully at this stage.*

'Centralize the hardtop on to the windscreen and ensure that the front sealing rubber fits down snugly and evenly. With the hard-top pushed forward as far as possible, adjust the front toggle links to give an adequate tension to the over-centre action; this is achieved by trial. Tighten the bolts securing the toggles to the hardtop. Fasten the toggle links and apply the safety catches.

'Loosen the hardtop side securing bolts and check that the quarter-panel sealing rubber is correctly positioned to pull down on to the car body.

'Whilst pressing down on the rear of the hardtop, examine the gap between the two side brackets. Determine the quantity of washers necessary to fill this gap and fit one less than this. Repeat this on the other side of the car.

'Keeping the rest of the hardtop centralized, tighten the hardtop side securing bolts fully. With pressure applied downwards on the rear of the hardtop, tighten the anchor-plate securing bolts.

'Final check of the correct hardtop position is obtained by winding up the door windows. A gap of approximately $\frac{6}{16}$ in. (8 mm) should exist between the rear vertical edge of the door windows and the quarter-light channel; adjustment may be achieved by loosening the side securing bolts and moving the hardtop forward or to the rear, as required. Check also that an even and adequate seal is made between the window and the hardtop rubber. Re-tighten the side securing bolts and carefully check the door opening and closing actions.'

Accessories in North America

In North America Dynoplastic's 'Royal Coachman' Landau hardtop for the MGB is similar in shape to the standard B.M.C.

hardtop. Made of fibre glass of double shell insulated construction it has an elegant exterior finish of embossed vinyl-leather.

Some of the Amco accessories are useful; the grille guard, for instance, is relatively inexpensive, while for the interior of the car anyone who wants an added radio speaker might well find the Amco console solves the difficulty of where to fit it. The console fits on top of the gearbox tunnel and incorporates an armrest which pulls up to reveal a convenient glove box.

In Germany and Austria thief-proof steering-lock devices are necessary before a car can be registered and licensed, and cars manufactured for export are already fitted with steering locks, but anyone who has to habitually leave his car unattended may find this a good extra to fit.

For the long-legged driver an extra length ($1\frac{1}{2}$ in.) steering column is available, while anyone who wants to give a little extra sparkle to the appearance of the 'B' may find the chrome spoked wheels worth fitting.

Overdrive and automatic gearbox

The ·802 Laycock de Normanville overdrive is an optional extra especially useful for motorway cruising and helps relieve stress and strain on the driver as well as on the engine. It reduces wear and maintenance and provides a bonus in the form of petrol saving as well as providing an extra gear between third and top which can be engaged instantly by the flip of a switch. Like most 'optionals' it is best to purchase a car with the overdrive already fitted, for it is less expensive this way. The automatic gearbox is an optional on GHN4 and GHD4 cars only, but, as with the Laycock overdrive, it is best to buy a car with the unit already fitted.

Fitting a radio

Provision is made for the radio to fit in the centre of the facia. This entails removing the radio blanking panel by releasing two clips on the rear of the panel. To gain access to the rear of the facia and the two clips, the speaker housing must be removed.

Most radio kits contain all the required parts for easy installation as well as an instruction sheet on fitting procedure. It is essential, however, whichever radio is being fitted, to ensure that the instructions regarding the polarity are rigidly observed, otherwise the transistors may be damaged.

The front-wing fitting position for the aerial on the GT is 10 in. forward of the chrome strip and $3\frac{3}{4}$ in. from the inner edge of the wing as measured from the wing beading. If an electrically-operated retractable aerial is to be fitted the measurement should be $10\frac{1}{4}$ in.

from the chrome strip and 4¾ in. from the inner edge of the wing.

To fit an aerial to the tourer, drill a ⅞ in. hole in the front wing (driver's side) 3¾ in. from the inner edge of the wing as measured from the wing beading and 7-5/16 in. from the front of the windscreen pillar.

To fit the aerial it is necessary to remove the mud-splash panel by taking out the seven retaining bolts. When the aerial is in position remove the blanking grommet in the body panel which will be found 4 in. below the aerial hole. Make a hole in the grommet and run the aerial lead through it and up to the requisite socket in the radio.

The speaker unit fits into the speaker housing and the housing can be removed from the car by taking the screws from each side of the unit and pulling the carpet away from the base. When this has been done pull the housing towards the gear lever, when it will become free and can be lifted out.

The speaker is held in the housing by four retaining studs and is quite simple to fit. The speaker lead can be led through the large aperture forward of the speaker-housing position and up to the radio.

It is essential to have the electrical system correctly suppressed and capacitors of 1 m f d must be attached to the following points: (a) the SW terminal of the ignition coil (white lead) with the body of the capacitors earthed to one of the coil mounting bolts; (b) the dynamo output terminal (brown lead with yellow tracer) with the body of the capacitor earthed to the dynamo rear-mounting bolt; (c) to the petrol pump which is mounted on the right-hand side of the chassis forward of the rear wheel. Connect the capacitors to the feed terminal (white lead) with the body earthed to the pump-mounting bracket.

When earthing capacitors it is essential to remove all rust and corrosion and to clean down to the bare metal.

Even when a radio is installed by experts certain static influences during reception may be noticed. Earth straps between the body and bonnet have been found useful in reducing some of this interference. The braking system is another source of certain static influences and a small amount of graphite powder in the rear brake-shoe locating slots has been found to help.

Steering wheels

Alloy-spoked wood-rim steering wheels are available from most accessory shops, but some of them, particularly those manufactured from a springy cane material, are a potential danger, for in the event of a bad crash the cane has been known to come unwrapped from

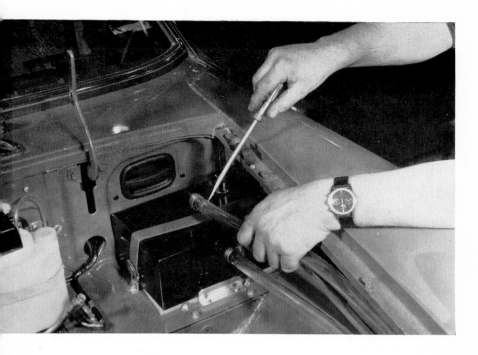

12 An oil spill tank is demanded for most race meetings

13 A tourer fitted with an auxiliary tank in the boot (note the connecting pipes)

14 *Above* 'The Bermuda' is one of many proprietary hardtops available

15 *Right* 'Roof windows' ensure a well-lit interior

16 *Below* The Tudor Webasto sun roof makes the GT version a great all-weather car

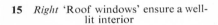

the steering wheel and result in a dangerous sharp projection some 9 in. long. If a wood-rim steering wheel is purchased be sure that the wood is securely riveted every two inches around the perimeter of the wheel, and that the wood is not of a springy-cane nature. Many drivers prefer the padded leather-covered type of steering wheel which transmits less road shock than the wooden type.

Anyone who is rallying or racing should consider Minilite wheels. Precision gravity cast in Magnesium Elektron C* which conforms to B.S.I. standards, they have many virtues, not the least of them being their great strength-to-weight ratio. Minilite have a a great capacity for shock absorption, while the special aerofoil spoke shape helps reduce brake temperature and although the wheels are rather more expensive than spoked wheels the extra financial outlay for anyone who is renewing a set of wheels for racing purposes might be worthwhile.

Optional extras can be obtained from the B.M.C. Service Department at Cowley, but approved accessories normally have to be obtained from the appropriate manufacturer or their agents. When ordering B.M.C. accessories or parts for your MG always quote the engine and chassis number.

While new parts and standard service replacement parts are obtainable from B.M.C. Service at Cowley, competitions spares which are prefixed by the letter C can only be obtained through the B.M.C. Special Tuning Department at Abingdon, Berkshire (phone Abingdon 251). If parts are ordered through a local garage unused to dealing with competition spares it is advisable to point out the fact that they must be obtained from Abingdon, otherwise unnecessary delay may ensue.

---

* Composition approximately 91% magnesium, 8% aluminium and traces of zinc and manganese.

K

CHAPTER 11

FAMILY RELATIONS

According to old music-hall jokes family relations can be aggravating and troublesome. This hardly applies to other models in the MG range although purists will dismiss the MG version of the B.M.C. 1100 range as not being sporting. They may consider that running MGBs as police cars is also not sporting but that is what several forces do! They have, as well as the usual police radio equipment, special police-checked speedometers, heavy-duty batteries and 11 AC-type alternators. The cars are standard in respect of power, the principal difference from the standard MGB being the special rear springs AHH 7346 which are used with the front springs AHH 5789 to give a feeling of greater stability but a slightly harder ride than the standard springs.

The MGC

Available in GT or tourer form the external appearance of the MGC is virtually the same as the 'B' except for its slightly raised bonnet. However, the 'C' has a six-cylinder 2912 cc engine and also torsion-bar suspension at the front. The body flooring is modified and considerably strengthened in comparison to the 'B' to get extra support and accommodate the cross-member which accepts the rear end of the torsion bars. Despite their similarity the bodies are not interchangeable and it is virtually impossible to convert one type to the other.

What are the advantages of torsion-bar suspension? Torsion bars are an efficient way of utilizing metal for suspension purposes and help towards saving a little front-end weight, though this is rather balanced by the extra weight of body strengthening to hold the bars. However, the weight is more generally distributed and their use means a less cluttered front end. In addition, a more accurate adjustment of the vehicle's front height is possible and any further settlement can be compensated throughout the life of the car should it be necessary. Torsion-bar suspension also gives better steering and added directional stability with less roll tendency (due to a steadier weight transference on cornering). There is also considerably less frontal dip when braking hard.

The fact that the 'C' has been given torsion-bar suspension is certainly not a reflection on the MGB, the torsion bars are fitted because of the added front end weight, coil springs really proving an inadequate suspension method for a modern sports car with the heavier frontal weight due to a six-cylinder unit.

While the MGC has a semi-floating tubed rear axle the same as the MGB GT, the rear-axle ratio of the MGC fitted with a manual gearbox is 3·307, whereas the GT has a ratio of 3·909.

The car has a new six-cylinder overhead valve, water-cooled engine, with a sturdy bottom end which has seven main bearings. The bore size is 3·282 in. and the stroke 3·5 in., and with a compression ratio of 9·0:1 the engine produces, in standard trim, 145 b h p at 5500 rev/min and over 200 b h p in competition trim.

It should be noted that the same flange-type extra-capacity petrol tanks which can be fitted to the MGB GT will also fit the MGC and with a little added work also to the tourer version of the 'B'.

Early independent road tests of the MGC found it disappointing in some respects but doubtless the Development Department at Abingdon will sort these out, particularly if the car is used by the Competitions Department in major events.

The Mark III Midget

Although the 'C' type is the latest of the MG marque, the MG Midget in its 1275 cc form is still competitive in its category. It is nearly 40 years since the first 'M'-type Midgets (847 cc) went into production (April 1929) and were successful the following year, when five of them achieved victory in the Brooklands Double Twelve Race; the Midgets of today are still successful in rallies and races.

The power output of the Mark III Midget is 65 b h p at 6000 rev/min in standard trim with an 8·8–1 compression ratio and a maximum torque of 72 lb ft at 3000 rev/min. The bore is 2·78 in. and the stroke 3·20 in., producing a cubic capacity per cylinder of 77·9 cc. The clutch is of the latest 6 in. diaphragm-spring type. Suspension is by semi-elliptic springs on the rear, while the independent front suspension is of the wishbone coil-spring type. The brakes are 8¼ in. diameter self-adjusting discs with 7 in. diameter drums on the rear.

Many competition spares are available for the Midget and the engine is capable of producing over 100 b h p.

The reputation of the MG marque is fiercely guarded by the management and workers at the Abingdon factory, aided by close liaison with the B.M.C. Competitions Department which is also housed there. Provided that the factory is allowed to retain its own character and is not completely swallowed up into the Leyland complex, MG sports cars should continue to attract ready sales amongst enthusiasts.

APPENDIX I

IDENTIFICATION DATA

Model	Commencing		Finishing	
	Car No.	Engine No.	Car No.	Engine No.
†MGB Tourer	G–HN3–101	18G/U/101 18GA/U/101 18GB/U/101	18GB/U/138360	18G/U/31121 18GA/U/17500 18GB/U/90942
	G–HN4–101	18GD/U/101 18GF/U/101		
†MGB GT	G–HD3– 71933 G–HD4	18GB/U/101		

Vehicle Identification
Serial Number Prefix Letter Code

The car number prefix comprises a series of letters and numbers, presenting in code the make, the engine type, the body type, the series, and, where applicable, left-hand drive.

1st Prefix letter—Name	2nd Prefix letter—Engine type
G—M.G.	H

3rd Prefix letter—Body type

N—2-seater Tourer
† D—Coupe or GT

4th Prefix—Series of model	5th Prefix (used to denote car is different to standard right-hand drive)
3—3rd Series	L—Left-hand drive

Code Example

G–H N 3–1 0 1

            Serial number
            3rd series
            2-seater Tourer
            'B'-type engine
            MG

Always quote these prefixes with Car Serial Numbers

Power Unit Identification
Serial Number Prefix Code

The engine number prefix comprises a series of letters and numbers, presenting in code the cubic capacity and make, the ancillaries fitted, and the type of compression.

1st Prefix Group—Cubic capacity, make, and type

1st Prefix number: 18—1800 cc
1st Prefix letter: G—MG

2nd Prefix Group—Gearbox and ancillaries

U—Centre gear change
R—Overdrive
RC—Automatic gearbox

3rd Group—Compression and serial number

H—High compression ⎱
L—Low compression ⎰ and serial number of unit

Code Example

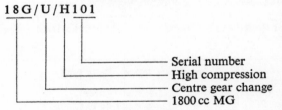

18G/U/H101

Serial number
High compression
Centre gear change
1800 cc MG

Always quote these prefixes with Engine Serial Numbers

APPENDIX II

GENERAL DATA

TECHNICAL DATA

(18G/18GA)

(18GB/18GD see page 153)

Engine

Type	18G, 18GA
Number of cylinders	4
Bore	3·16 in. (80·26 mm)
Stroke	3·5 in. (89 mm)
Capacity	1798 cc (109·8 in³)
Combustion-chamber volume (valves fitted)	42·5 to 43·5 cc (2·59 to 2·65 in³)
Firing order	1, 3, 4, 2
Valve operation	Overhead by push-rod
Compression ratio: HC	8·8:1
LC	8·0:1
Compression pressure: HC	160 lb/in² (11·25 kg/cm²)
LC	130 lb/in² (9·15 kg/cm²)
Torque: HC	110 lb ft (15·2 kg m) at 3,000 rev/min
LC	105 lb ft (14·5 kg m) at 3,000 rev/min
b h p	HC 95 (LC 91) at 5,400
b m e p	152 at 3,100
Octane rating	HC 98+, LC 93+
Safe maximum rev/min	6,000
Engine idle speed (approx.)	500 rev/min
Oversize bore: First	·010 in. (·254 mm)
Max.	·040 in. (1·016 mm)

Crankshaft

Main journal diameter	2·1265 to 2·127 in. (54·01 to 54·02 mm)
Crankpin journal diameter	1·8759 to 1·8764 in. (47·648 to 47·661 mm)
Crankshaft end-thrust	Taken on thrust-washers at centre main bearing
Crankshaft end-float	·002 to ·003 in. (·051 to ·076 mm)

Main bearings

Number and type	Three thinwall
Material	Steel-backed copper-lead
Length	1⅛ in. (28·5 mm)
Diametrical clearance	·001 to ·0027 in. (·0254 to ·068 mm)
Undersizes	—·010, —·020, —·030 and —·040 in. (—·254, —·508, —·762 and —1·016 mm)

Connecting rods

Type   Angular-split big-end, split clamp
                                        small-end
Length between centres   6·5 in. (165·1 mm)

Big-end bearings

Type   Shell
Material   Steel-backed copper-lead
Length   ·995 to 1·005 in. (25·2 to 25·52 mm)
Diametrical clearance   ·001 to ·0027 in. (·0254 to ·068 mm)
Undersizes   —·010, —·020, —·030 and —·040 in.
                                        (—·254, —·508, —·762 and —1·016
                                        mm)
End-float on crankpin (nominal)   ·008 to ·012 in. (·20 to ·30 mm)

Pistons

Type   Aluminium solid skirt
Clearance in cylinder: Top   ·0036 to ·0045 in. (·091 to ·121 mm)
                       Bottom   ·0018 to ·0024 in. (·045 to ·060 mm)
Number of rings   4 (3 compression, 1 oil control)
Width of ring grooves:
  Top, Second and Third   ·064 to ·065 in. (1·625 to 1·651 mm)
  Oil control   ·1578 to ·1588 in. (4·008 to 4·033 mm)
Gudgeon pin bore   ·7501 to ·7503 in. (19·052 to 19·057 mm)

Piston rings

Compression
  Type: Top,   Parallel ⎫ cast iron—molybdenum
        Second and Third   Tapered ⎭ filled
  Width: Top, Second and Third   ·0615 to ·0625 in. (1·562 to 1·587 mm)
  Fitted gap: Top, Second and Third   ·012 to ·017 in. (·304 to ·431 mm)
  Ring to groove clearance:
    Top, Second and Third   ·0015 to ·0035 in. (·038 to ·088 mm)
Oil control
  Type   Slotted scraper
  Width   ·1552 to ·1562 in. (3·94 to 3·96 mm)
  Fitted gap   ·012 to ·017 in. (·304 to ·431 mm)
  Ring to groove clearance   ·0016 to ·0036 in. (·04 to ·09 mm)

Gudgeon pin

Type   Semi-floating
Fit in piston   Free fit at 20°C (68°F)
Diameter (outer)   ·7499 to ·7501 in. (19·04 to 19·05 mm)

Camshaft

Journal diameters: Front   1·78875 to 1·78925 in. (45·424 to
                                        45·437 mm)
                   Centre   1·72875 to 1·72925 in. (43·910 to
                                        43·923 mm)
                   Rear   1·62275 to 1·62325 in. (41·218 to
                                        41·230 mm)

Camshaft—cont.

Bearing liner inside diameter (reamed after fitting):	Front	1·79025 to 1·79075 in. (45·472 to 45·485 mm)
	Centre	1·73025 to 1·73075 in. (43·948 to 43·961 mm)
	Rear	1·62425 to 1·62475 in. (41·256 to 41·269 mm)

Diametrical clearance	·001 to ·002 in. (·0254 to ·0508 mm)
End-thrust	Taken on locating plate
End-float	·003 to ·007 in. (·076 to ·178 mm)
Cam lift	·250 in. (6·35 mm)
Drive	Chain and sprocket from crankshaft
Timing chain	$\frac{3}{8}$ in. (9·52 mm) pitch × 52 pitches

Tappets

Type	Barrel with flat base
Outside diameter	$\frac{13}{16}$ in. (20·64 mm)
Length	2·293 to 2·303 in. (58·25 to 58·5 mm)

Rocker gear

Rocker shaft
Length	$14\frac{1}{32}$ in. (356 mm)
Diameter	·624 to ·625 in. (15·85 to 15·87 mm)

Rocker arm
Bore	·7485 to ·7495 in. (19·01 to 19·26 mm)
Rocker-arm bush inside diameter	·6255 to ·626 in. (15·8 to 15·9 mm)
Ratio	1·4:1

Cylinder head

Cylinder-head depth	$3\frac{11}{64} {}^{+\,·015\text{in.}}_{-\,·000\text{in.}}$ $\left(80·6 {}^{+\,·400\text{mm}}_{-\,·000\text{mm}}\right)$
Thickness of cylinder-head gasket	·023 in. (·584 mm) compressed
Capacity of cylinder-head gasket	3·208 cc
Capacity of combustion space	42·5/43·5 cc (valves fitted)
Capacity of piston head below block face (including capacity of piston concavity)	HC 10·87 cc (LC 17·43 cc)
Capacity of plug centre hole	HC 6·25 cc (LC 12·8 cc) ·2 cc
Inlet and exhaust manifold gasket	Part no. 1G 2417
Valve-seat angle in cylinder head	45°

Valves

Seat angle: Inlet and exhaust	$45\frac{1}{2}°$
Head diameter: Inlet	1·562 to 1·567 in. (38·67 to 38·80 mm)
Exhaust	1·343 to 1·348 in. (34·11 to 34·23 mm)
Stem diameter: Inlet	·3422 to ·3427 in. (8·68 to 8·69 mm)
Exhaust	·3417 to ·3422 in. (8·660 to 8·661 mm)
Stem to guide clearance: Inlet	·0015 to ·0025 in. (·0381 to ·0778 mm)
Exhaust	·002 to ·003 in. (·0508 to ·0762 mm)
Valve lift: Inlet and exhaust	·3645 in. (9·25 mm)

Valve guides

Length: Inlet	1⅝ in. (41·275 mm)
Exhaust	2¹³⁄₁₆ in. (55·95 mm)
Outside diameter: Inlet and exhaust	·5635 to ·5640 in. (14·30 to 14·32 mm)
Inside diameter: Inlet and exhaust	·3442 to ·3447 in. (8·73 to 8·74 mm)
Fitted height above head:	
Inlet and exhaust	⅝ in. (15·875 mm)
Interference fit in head:	
Inlet and exhaust	·0005 to ·00175 in. (·012 to ·044 mm)

(Later cars)

Length: Inlet	1⅞ in. (47·63 mm)
Fitting Height above head: Inlet	¾ in. (19 mm)

Valve springs

Free length: Inner	1³¹⁄₃₂ in. (50·0 mm)
Outer	2⁹⁄₆₄ in. (54·4 mm)
Fitted length: Inner	1⁷⁄₁₆ in. (36·5 mm)
Outer	1⁹⁄₁₆ in. (39·7 mm)
Load at fitted length: Inner	28 to 32 lb (12·7 to 14·5 kg)
Outer	72 lb (32·7 kg)
Load at top of lift: Inner	48 to 52 lb (21·7 to 23·6 kg)
Outer	117 lb (53 kg)
Valve crash speed	6,200 rev/min

Valve timing

Timing marks	Dimples on camshaft and crankshaft wheels
Rocker clearance: Running	·015 in. (·38 mm) cold
Timing	·021 in. (·533 mm)
Inlet valve: Opens	16° btdc
Closes	56° abdc
Exhaust valve: Opens	51° bbdc
Closes	21° atdc

Engine lubrication

System	Wet sump, pressure-fed
System pressure: Running	Between 50 and 80 lb/in² (3·51 and 5·6 kg/cm²)
Idling	Between 10 and 25 lb/in² (·7 and 1·7 kg/cm²)
Oil pump	Hobourn-Eaton or Concentric rotor
Capacity	3¼ gal/min at 2,000 rev/min
Oil filter	Tecalemit full-flow felt element
By-pass valve opens	13 to 17 lb/in² (·9 to 1·1 kg/cm²)
Oil-pressure relief valve	70 lb/in² (4·9 kg/cm²)
Relief valve spring:	
Free length	3 in. (76·2 mm)
Fitted length	2⁵⁄₃₂ in. (54·7 mm)
Load at fitted length	15·5 to 16·5 lb (7·0 to 7·4 kg)

Fuel system

Carburetters	Twin SU Type HS4
Choke diameter	1½ in. (38·1 mm)
Jet size	·090 in. (2·2 mm)
Needles	No. 5 (Standard), No. 6 (Rich), 21 (Weak)
Piston spring	Red
Air cleaners	Cooper paper element
Fuel pump	
Type (Early cars)	SU electric HP
Minimum flow	7 gal/hr (31·8 litres/hr, 8·4 US gal/hr)
Suction head	2 ft 6 in. (76·2 cm)
Delivery head	4 ft (122 cm)
Minimum starting voltage	9·5 volts
Type (Later cars)	SU electric AUF 300
Minimum flow	15 gal/hr (68·2 litre/hr, 18 US gal/hr)
Suction head	18 in. (457 mm)

Cooling System

Type	Pressurized. Pump-impeller- and fan-assisted
Thermostat setting	
Standard	74°C (165°F)
Hot climate	74°C (165°F)
Cold climate	82°C (180°F)
Pressure cap	7 lb (3·175 kg)
Fan blades	3 at 24°
Fan belt: Width	⅜ in. (9·5 mm)
Outside length	35½ in. (90·2 cm)
Thickness	5/16 in. (7·9 mm)
Tension	½ in. (12·8 mm) movement
Type of pump	Centrifugal
Pump drive	Belt from crankshaft pulley

Ignition system

Coil	HA12 (oil-filled)
Resistance at 20°C (68°F):	
Primary winding	3·1 to 3·5 ohms (cold)
Consumption: Ignition switch on	3·9 amps
At 2,000 rev/min	1·4 amps
Distributor	25D4
Rotation of rotor	Anti-clockwise
Cam form	4-cylinder high-lift
Cam-closed period	60°±3°
Cam-open period	30°±3°
Automatic advance	Centrifugal and vacuum

Serial Number	*Serial Number*
40897 (*HC*)	40916 (*LC*)

Distributor—cont.

Automatic advance commences	400 rev/min	400 rev/min
Maximum advance		
(crankshaft degrees)	20° at 2,200 rev/min	24° at 4,400 rev/min
Vacuum advance	20° at 13 in. (33·3 cm)	16° at 12 in. (30·5 cm)
(crankshaft degrees)	Hg	Hg
Decelerating check (crankshaft	20° at 2,200 rev/min	24° at 4,400 rev/min
degrees, engine rev/min)	15° at 1,600 rev/min	18° at 3,000 rev/min
	9° at 900 rev/min	9° at 1,000 rev/min
	6° at 700 rev/min	8° at 800 rev/min
	6° at 600 rev/min	6° at 600 rev/min

Contact-point gap setting	·014 to ·016 in. (·35 to ·40 mm)
Breaker spring tension	18 to 24 oz. (510 to 680 gm)
Condenser capacity	·18 to ·24 mF
Timing marks	Pointer on timing chain case and notch on crankshaft pulley
Static ignition timing: HC	10° b t d c (98/100-octane fuel)
LC	8° b t d c (95/97-octane fuel)
Stroboscopic ignition timing: HC	14° b t d c at 600 rev/min
LC	12° b t d c at 600 rev/min
Suppressors	Lucas W55 Type L2. Fitted in plug leads
Sparking plugs	Champion N–9Y
Size	14 mm ¾ in. (19·0 mm) reach
Gap	·024 to ·026 in. (·625 to ·660 mm)

Clutch

Make and type	Borg & Beck 8 in. DS.G diaphragm spring
Diaphragm spring colour	Dark blue
Clutch-plate diameter	8 in. (20·32 cm)
Facing material	Wound yarn
Number of damper springs	6
Damper spring load	110 to 120 lb (49·8 to 54·3 kg)
Damper spring colour	Black/light green
Clutch-release bearing	Graphite (MY3D)
Clutch fluid	Lockheed Disc Brake Fluid (Series II)

Gearbox and Overdrive (up to but not including Series iv)

Number of forward gears	4	
Gearbox ratios: Reverse	4·76:1	
First	3·64:1	
Second	2·21:1	
Third	1·37:1	
Fourth	1·00:1	
Overdrive ratio	·802:1	
Overall gear ratios: Reverse	18·588:1	
First	14·214:1	
Second	8·656:1	*Overdrive*
Third	5·369:1	4·306:1
Fourth	3·909:1	3·135:1

Gearbox and Overdrive—*cont.*

Top gear speed per 1,000 rev/min:
  Standard   17·9 mile/h (27·3 km/h)
  Overdrive   22·3 mile/h (35·5 km/h)
Speedometer gear ratio: Standard   9/28
                    Overdrive   5/16
Synchromesh hub springs:
  Free length $\frac{1}{2}$ in. (12·7 mm)
  Fitted length $\frac{5}{16}$ in. (7·9 mm)
  Load at fitted length   4 to 5 lb (1·8 to 2·2 kg)
Shaft and reverse plunger
  detent-springs: Free length $1\frac{3}{16}$ in. (30·16 mm)
              Fitted length $\frac{3}{4}$ in. (19·0 mm)
      Load at fitted length 18 to 20 lb (8·16 to 9·07 kg)
Reverse plunger spring:
  Free length   1 in. (25·4 mm)
  Fitted length $\frac{13}{16}$ in. (20·63 mm)
  Load at fitted length $91\frac{1}{4}$ to $92\frac{1}{4}$ lb. (41·4 to 41·9 kg)
Mainshaft second and third gear
  end-float   ·004 to ·006 in. (·102 to ·152 mm)
Laygear end-float   ·002 to ·003 in. (·051 to ·076 mm)
Overdrive
  Pump spring: Free length   2·000 in. (50·8 mm)
                Rate   11 lb in. (12·7 kg cm)
  Clutch spring: Free length   1·510 in. (38·3 mm)
                Rate   154 lb in. (178 kg cm)

Propeller shaft

Type   Open tubular, telescopic
Universal joints   Hardy Spicer needle roller
Angular movement   18° to 20°
Overall length:
  Fully extended: Standard $37\frac{7}{8}$ in. (81 cm)
             Overdrive $30\frac{3}{4}$ in. (78·1 cm)
  Fully compressed: Standard $30\frac{3}{16}$ in. (76·5cm)
             Overdrive $29\frac{1}{16}$ in. (74 cm)
Length of shaft assembly: Standard $26\frac{15}{32}$ in. (67 cm)
                Overdrive $25\frac{11}{32}$ in. (64·3 cm)
Tube diameter   2 in. (50·8 mm)

Rear axle

Type   Hypoid, three-quarter-floating
Ratio   3·909:1 (11/43)
Differential-bearing preload   ·002 in. (·05 mm) 'nip' per bearing
Pinion-bearing preload   7 to 9 lb in. (·8 to 1·0 kg m)
Backlash adjustment: Crown wheel Shims
                 Pinion   Head washer

Steering

Type   Rack and pinion
Steering-wheel diameter $16\frac{1}{2}$ in. (419·10 mm)

Steering—*cont*.

Turns—lock to lock   2·93
Turning circle   32 ft (9·75 m)
Universal joint   Hardy Spicer KO518, GB166
Pinion end-float   ·002 to ·005 in. (·05 to ·12 mm)
Damper end-float   ·0005 to ·003 in. (·012 to ·076 mm)
                                      (unladen)
Toe-in $\frac{1}{16}$ to $\frac{3}{32}$ in. (1·5 to 2·3 mm) (unladen)
Angle of outer wheel with inner wheel
  at 20°   18°

Front suspension

Type   Independent. Coil spring and wishbone.
Spring: Coil diameter (mean)   3·238 in. (82·2 mm)
        Free height   9·9$\pm\frac{1}{16}$ in. (251·4$\pm$1·5 mm)
        Static length at 1,030 lb
          (467·2 kg) load   7$\pm\frac{1}{32}$ in. (178$\pm$·8 mm)
        Number of free coils   7·5
Camber angle   Nominal 1° positive ($+\frac{1}{4}°, -1\frac{1}{4}°$)
                                        $=1\frac{1}{4}°$ positive, $\frac{1}{4}°$ negative
Castor angle   Nominal 7° ($+\frac{1}{4}°, -2°)=5°$ to $7\frac{1}{4}°$ $\Big\}$(unladen)
King-pin inclination   Nominal 8° ($+1°, -\frac{3}{4}°)=7\frac{1}{4}°$ to 9°
Dampers   Armstrong piston type
  Arm centres   8 in. (203·2 mm)
Wheel-bearing end-float   ·002 to ·004 in. (·05 to ·10 mm)

Rear suspension

Type   Semi-elliptic leaf spring
Number of spring leaves   5+bottom plate. Interleaving 1/2, 2/3,
                                        3/4
Width of spring leaves   1$\frac{3}{4}$ in. (44·4 mm)
Gauge of leaves
  Early cars $\frac{7}{32}$ in. (5·56 mm)
  Later cars   3 at $\frac{7}{32}$ in. (5·6 mm), 3 at $\frac{3}{16}$ in. (4·8 mm)
Working load ($\pm$15 lb [7 kg])
  Early cars   400 lb (181·5 kg)
  Later cars   450 lb (204·1 kg)
Dampers   Armstrong piston type
  Arm centres   5$\frac{1}{4}$ in. (133 mm)

Electrical equipment

System   12 volt, positive earth (up to Series **IV**)
  Charging system   Current/voltage control
  Batteries—two 6 volt   Lucas SG9E or STGZ9E
                                      Lucas BT9E or BTZ9E—later cars
    Capacity: 10 hour rate   51 amp-hr
              20 hour rate   58 amp-hr
    Plates per cell   9
Electrolyte to fill one cell   1 pint (570 cc: 1·2 US pints)

Regulator   RB340
Voltage setting at 3,000 rev/min:
  10°C (50°F)   14·7 to 15·7 volts
  20°C (68°F)   14·5 to 15·5 volts
  30°C (86°F)   14·3 to 15·3 volts
  40°C (104°F)   14·1 to 15·1 volts
Current setting at 4,000 rev/min   22 amps
Cut-out relay: Cut-in voltage   12·7 to 13·3 volts
       Drop-off voltage   9·5 to 11·0 volts

Dynamo   C40/1. 12 volt two-brush
Maximum output   22 amps
Cut-in speed   1,585 rev/min at 13·5 volts
Field resistance   6·0 ohmns
Brush-spring tension   22 to 25 oz (623 to 708 gm)
Drive   Belt from crankshaft
Drive adjustment   Swinging link on dynamo

Starter motor   M418G four-brush inertia type
Lock torque   17 lb ft (2·35 kg m) at 340 amps
Torque at 1,000 rev/min   8 lb ft (1·11 kg m) at 250 to 270 amps
Brush-spring tension   32 to 40 oz (907 to 1133 gm)
Starter gear ratio   13·3:1

Wiper motor   DR 3A single speed
Drive to wheelboxes   Rack and cable
Armature end-float   ·008 to ·012 in. (·20 to ·30 mm)
Running current   2·7 to 3·4 amps
Wiping speed   45 to 50 cycles per minute
Angle of wipe   106° (earlier cars 150°)

Horns
Type   9H 12 volt
Maximum current consumption   3½ amps

Brakes
Type   Lockheed hydraulic. Disc front,
                                             drum rear
Brake fluid   Lockheed Disc Brake Fluid (Series II)

Front
Disc diameter   10¾ in. (27·3 cm)
Pad material   Don 55
Swept area   203·2 in² (1311 cm²)
Pad area (std)   20·0 in²

Rear
Drum diameter   10 in. (25·4 cm)
Lining material   Don 24
Swept area   106·8 in² (683·9 cm²)
Lining area   67·2 in²
Lining dimensions   9 7/16 × 1¾ × 3/16 in. (240 × 44·4 × 4·76 mm)

Brake-cylinder diameter
Front $2\frac{1}{8}$ in. (53·97 mm) dia
Rear   ·80 in. (20·32 mm) dia

Wheels
Type   Ventilated disc, 4-stud fixing
                                         Wire (optional)
Size: Disc   4J × 14 GT 5J × 14
    Wire (optional) and 60 spoke $4\frac{1}{2}$J × 14

Tyres
Standard:
  Size   5·60 — 14 tubed C41
  Rolling radius   11·65 in. (29·5 cm) at 30 mile/h (48 km/h)
Optional:
  Size   155 — 14 SP
Standard tyres:
  Pressures (set cold):
    Front   18 lb/in^2 (1·3 kg/cm^2)
    Rear   18 lb/in^2 (1·3 kg/cm^2)
  Sustained speeds in excess of
    90 mile/h (145 km/h)
    Front   24 lb/in^2 (1·7 kg/cm^2)
    Rear   24 lb/in^2 (1·7 kg/cm^2)
Optional tyres (SP):
  Pressures (set cold):
    Front   21 lb/in^2 (1·5 kg/cm^2)
    Rear   24 lb/in^2 (1·7 kg/cm^2)
  Sustained speeds in excess of
    90 mile/h (145 km/h):
    Front   27 lb/in^2 (1·9 kg/cm^2)
    Rear   31 lb/in^2 (2·2 kg/cm^2)

Note—Rear tyre pressures may be increased by 2 lb/in^2 (·14 kg/cm^2) with advantage when touring with a laden boot.

Capacities
Fuel tank: Early cars   10 gallons (45·4 litres, 12 US gallons)
    Later cars   12 gallons (54 litres, 14 US gallons)
Cooling system $9\frac{1}{2}$ pints (5·4 litres, 11·4 US pints)
Heater $\frac{1}{2}$ pint (·28 litre, ·6 US pint)
Engine sump $7\frac{1}{2}$ pints (4·26 litres, 9 US pints)
Oil cooler $\frac{3}{4}$ pint (·42 litre, ·9 US pint)
Gearbox $4\frac{1}{2}$ pints (2·56 litres, 5·6 US pints)
Gearbox and overdrive $5\frac{1}{3}$ pints (3·36 litres, 6 US pints)
Rear axle $2\frac{1}{4}$ pints (1·28 litres, 2·75 US pints)
Steering rack $\frac{1}{3}$ pint (·19 litre, ·39 US pint)

Dimensions
Overall length   12 ft $8\frac{1}{2}$ in. (3·874 m)

Dimensions—*cont.*

Overall length (with overriders)	12 ft 9$\frac{3}{8}$ in. (3·897 m)
Overall width	4 ft 11$\frac{15}{16}$in. (152·3 cm)
Overall height (hood erected)	4 ft 1$\frac{3}{8}$ in. (125·4 cm)
Ground clearance (minimum)	5 in. (12·7 cm)
Wheelbase	7 ft 7 in. (231·1 cm)
Track: Front (disc wheels)	4 ft 1 in. (124·4 cm)
Rear (disc wheels)	4 ft 1$\frac{1}{4}$ in. (125 cm)
Front (wire wheels)	4 ft 1$\frac{1}{4}$ in. (125 cm)
Rear (wire wheels)	4 ft 1$\frac{1}{4}$ in. (125 cm)

Weights

Unladen weight	1,920 lb (871 kg)
Engine (dry, with clutch)	358 lb (163·3 kg) approx
Gearbox	78 lb (35·5 kg) approx
Rear axle: Disc wheels	117$\frac{1}{2}$ lb (53·26 kg) approx
Wire wheels	123 lb (55·79 kg) approx

Front and rear springs

Part no.	Type	Rate (lb/in.)	Working load (lb)	Deflection at working load (in.)	Fitted height (in.)	
AHH 6451	Coil	348	1030	2·965	7·0	
AHH 5789	Coil	480	1193	24·9	6·6	Fitted to GT
C–AHT 21	Coil	480	1193	2·49	6·14	Fitted to tourers from
AHH 7080	Leaf	93	450 (flat)	4·97		Car no. 11313
AHH 6453	Leaf	99	400 (flat)	4·04		Fitted to tourers prior to Car no. 11313
C–AHH 8343	Leaf	100	375 (flat)	3·75		
AHC 31	Leaf	99	510 (flat)	3.20		Fitted to GT
AHH 7346	Leaf	124	542 (flat)	4·37		
C–AHT 20	Leaf	124	542 (flat)	3·37		

(18GB and 18GD)

The following information is applicable to the 18GB/18GD-engined cars and should be used in conjunction with the preceding specification for the 18G/18GA-engined car.

Engine

Type	18GB
Weight	std 418 lb (o/d 436 lb)

Main bearings

Number and type	5 thin-wall
Length: Front, centre and rear	1$\frac{1}{8}$ in. (28·5 mm)
Intermediate	$\frac{7}{8}$ in. (22·23 mm)

Connecting rods

Type	Angular-split big-end, bushed small-end

L

Big-end bearings
Length   ·775 to ·785 in. (19·68 to 19·94 mm)

Pistons
Gudgeon-pin bore   ·8126 to ·8129 (20·610 to 20·617 mm)

Gudgeon pin
Type   Fully floating
Fit in piston   ·0001 to ·00035 in. (·0025 to ·007 mm)
Diameter (outer)   ·8124 to ·8127 (20·608 to 20·615 mm)

Rear axle (GT) and GHN3 tourers with wire wheels after chassis no. 129287
   and with disc wheels after no. 132463
Type   Hypoid, semi-floating

Wheels (GT)
Size: Disc   5J × 14 in.

Tyres (GT)
Size:
   Standard   5·60 × 14
   Optional   165 × 14 SP
   Standard tyres:
   Pressures (set cold):
      Front   20 lb/in² (1·4 kg/cm²)
      Rear   24 lb/in² (1·7 kg/cm²)
   Sustained speeds in excess of
      90 mile/h (145 km/h):
         Front   26 lb/in² (1·8 kg/cm²)
         Rear   30 lb/in² (2·1 kg/cm²)
Optional tyres:
   Pressures (set cold):
      Front   21 lb/in² (1·5 kg/cm²)
      Rear   24 lb/in² (1·7 kg/cm²)
   Sustained speeds in excess of
      90 mile/h (145 km/h):
         Front   28 lb/in² (2·0 kg/cm²)
         Rear   31 lb/in² (2·2 kg/cm²)

Capacities
Rear axle (semi-floating type) 1½ pints (·85 litres, 2 US gallons)

Dimensions
Overall height (GT)   4 ft 1¾ in. (126·3 cm)

Weights
Unladen weight (GT)   2,190 lb (993 kg)

1,843 cc engine

C/R	Flat top pistons	C/R	Concave top pistons
11·1:1	Vol. of cyl. head 37 c	9·82:1	Vol. of cyl. head 37 cc
10·6:1	Vol. of cyl. head 39 cc	9·5:1	Vol. of cyl. head 39 cc
10:1	Vol. of cyl. head 42 cc	9·0:1	Vol. of cyl. head 42 cc

The unswept cyl. vol. of a 1,843 cc engine (pistons ·025 from top of bore) is approx. 4·08 cc.

The volume of a competition type cyl. head casket is approx. 4·86 cc.

1,798 cc engine

C/R	Flat top pistons	C/R	Concave top pistons
11·1:1	Vol. of cyl. head 37 cc	(9·7) 10:1	Vol. of cyl. head 37 cc
10·5:1	Vol. of cyl. head 39 cc	(9·43) 9·5:1	Vol. of cyl. head 39 cc
(9·98):1 10:1	Vol. of cyl. head 42 cc	(8·98) 9·0:1	Vol. of cyl. head 42 cc

The unswept cyl. volume of a 1,798 cc engine (pistons ·025 from top of bore) is approx. 3·21 cc.

The volume of a standard piston concavity is approx. 6·25 cc.

TUNING DATA

18GF engine

Engine

Firing order	1, 3, 4, 2
Capacity	1798 cc (109·8 in²)
Compression ratio	8·8:1
Compression pressure	160 lb/in² (11·25 kg/cm²)
Idle speed	800 to 900 rev/min
Fast idle speed	1,300 to 1,400 rev/min
Valve-rocker clearance	·015 in. (·38 mm) set cold
Stroboscopic ignition timing	30° b t d c at 3,000 rev/min
Static ignition timing	t d c
Timing-mark location	Pointer on timing case, notch on crankshaft pulley

Distributor

Make	Lucas
Type	25 D4

Distributor—*cont.*
Serial number:
Contact-breaker gap   ·014 to ·016 in. (·35 to ·4 mm)
Rotation of rotor   Anti-clockwise
Dwell angle   57° to 63°
Condenser capacity   ·18 to ·24 mF

Centrifugal advance—Crankshaft degrees (Vacuum pipe disconnected)
0°   degrees at   500 to 700 rev/min
23°   degrees at   1,500 to 1,750 rev/min
30°+2° degrees at   3,000 rev/min

Vacuum advance
Starts   6 in. Hg
Finishes   13 in. Hg
Total crankshaft degrees   10°+2°

Sparking plugs
Make   Champion
Type   N–9Y
Gap   ·024 to ·026 in. (·625 to ·660 mm)

Ignition coil
Make   Lucas
Type   HA12
Resistance—primary   3·1 to 3·5 ohms at 20°C (68°F)

Consumption
Ignition on—standing   3·9 amps
          —at 2,000 rev/min   1·4 amps

Carburetter(s)
Make   SU
Type   Twin HS4
Choke diameter   1½ in. (38·1 mm)
Jet size   ·090 in. (2·2 mm)
Needle   FX
Piston spring   Red
Initial jet adjustment   12 flats from bridge

Exhaust emission
Exhaust gas analyser reading:
   At engine idle speed   4·5 to 5% CO
   Air-pump test speed   1,000 rev/min (engine)

APPENDIX III

TORQUE WRENCH SETTING

Engine

Main bearing nuts	70 lb ft (9·7 kg m)
Flywheel set screws	40 lb ft (5·5 kg m)
Gudgeon-pin clamp bolt	25 lb ft (3·4 kg m)
Big-end bolts	35 to 40 lb ft (4·8 to 5·5 kg m)
Cylinder-head nuts	45 to 50 lb ft (6·2 to 6·9 kg m)
Rocker bracket nuts	25 lb ft (3·4 kg m)
Oil pump to crankcase	14 lb ft (1·9 kg m)
Sump to crankcase	6 lb ft (·8 kg m)
Cylinder side-cover screws	2 lb ft (·28 kg m)
Second type—deep pressed cover	5 lb ft (·7 kg m)
Timing cover—$\frac{1}{4}$ in. screws	6 lb ft (·8 kg m)
Timing cover—$\frac{5}{16}$ in. screws	14 lb ft (1·9 kg m)
Rear plate—$\frac{5}{16}$ in. screws	20 lb ft (2·8 kg m)
Rear plate—$\frac{3}{8}$ in. screws	30 lb ft (4·1 kg m)
Water pump to crankcase	25 lb ft (3·5 kg m)
Water outlet elbow nuts	8 lb ft (1·1 kg m)
Rocker cover nuts	4 lb ft (·56 kg m)
Manifold nuts	25 lb ft (3·4 kg m)
Oil filter centre-bolt	15 lb ft (2·1 kg m)
Clutch to flywheel	25 to 30 lb ft (3·4 to 4·1 kg m)
Carburetter stud nuts	2 lb ft (·28 kg m)
Distributor clamp bolt (nut trapped)	4·16 lb ft (·57 kg m)
Distributor clamp nut (bolt trapped)	2·5 lb ft (·35 kg m)

Rear axle (three-quarter floating type)

Crown wheel to differential carrier	55 to 60 lb ft (7·6 to 8·3 kg m)
Differential-bearing cap	60 to 65 lb ft (8·3 to 8·9 kg m)
Pinion-bearing nut	135 to 140 lb ft (18·6 to 19·3 kg m)
Rear-brake-adjuster securing nuts	5 to 7 lb ft (·69 to ·97 kg m)
Bearing retaining nut	180 lb ft (24·8 kg m)

Rear axle (semi-floating type)

Half-shaft nut (semi-floating axle)	150 lb ft (20·75 kg m)
Differential-bearing cap bolts	50 to 55 lb ft (6·9 to 7·6 kg m)
Crown-wheel bolts	60 to 65 lb ft (8·3 to 8·9 kg m)
Pinion nut	135 to 145 lb ft (18·6 to 20 kg m)
Axle-shaft nut	150 lb ft (20·6 kg m) and aligned to next split-pin hole

Rear suspension

Rear shock-absorber bolts	40 lb ft (5·5 kg m)

Front suspension

Front shock-absorber bolt	45 lb ft (6·2 kg m)
Brake disc to hub	40 to 45 lb ft (5·5 to 6·2 kg m)
Brake calliper mounting	40 to 45 lb ft (5·5 to 6·2 kg m)
Bearing retaining nut	40 to 70 lb ft (5·5 to 9·7 kg m)
Cross-member to body	55 lb ft (7·6 kg m)

Steering

Steering-arm bolts	60 to 65 lb ft (8·3 to 8·9 kg m)
Steering-wheel nut	42 lb ft (5·8 kg m)
Steering tie-rod locknut	33·3 to 37·5 lb ft (4·6 to 5·2 kg m)
Steering lever ball joint nut	35 lb ft (4·8 kg m)
Steering universal joint bolt	20 lb ft (2·8 kg m)

Road wheels

Road-wheel nuts	60 to 62·5 lb ft (8·3 to 8·6 kg m)

APPENDIX IV

MAINTENANCE AND LUBRICATION

MAINTENANCE SUMMARY

Weekly

Inspect engine oil level, and top up as necessary.
Check water level in radiator, and top up if necessary.
Check battery and top up to correct levels.
Test tyre pressures.

3,000 miles (5000 km) or 3 months' service

1. *Engine*
   Top up carburetter piston dampers.
   Check the coolant level in radiator.
   Top up windscreen-washer bottle.
2. *Clutch*
   Check level of fluid in the hydraulic clutch master cylinder.
3. *Brakes*
   Check brakes, and adjust if necessary.
   Make visual inspection of brake lines and pipes.
   Check level of fluid in the hydraulic brake master cylinder.
4. *Electrical*
   Check batteries and top up to correct level.
5. *Lubrication*
   Check and top up engine-oil level.
   Change engine oil (if using monograde only).
   Lubricate all grease nipples (except steering rack and pinion).
6. *Wheels and tyres*
   Check tyre pressures.

6,000 miles (10000 km) or 6 months' service

1. *Engine*
   Top up carburetter piston dampers.
   Check fan-belt tension.
   Check air-pump belt tension (GF cars)
   Check valve-rocker clearances, and adjust if necessary.
   Check the coolant level in radiator.
   Top up windscreen-washer bottle.
   Check exhaust-emission (18GF cars only).

2. *Ignition*
  Check automatic retard and advance mechanism.
  Check distributor contact points, and adjust if necessary.
  Lubricate all distributor parts as necessary.
  Clean and adjust sparking plugs.
3. *Clutch*
  Check level of fluid in the hydraulic clutch master cylinder.
4. *Steering*
  Check wheel alignment, and adjust if necessary.
5. *Brakes*
  Check brakes, and adjust if necessary.
  Make visual inspection of brake lines and pipes.
  Check level of fluid in the hydraulic brake master cylinder.
  Inspect the disc-brake friction pads and renew if required.
6. *Electrical*
  Check battery cell specific gravity readings, and top up to correct level.
  Check all lamps for correct functioning.
7. *Lubrication*
  Change oil in engine.
  Lubricate dynamo end bearing.
  Top up gearbox, overdrive (if applicable), and rear-axle oil levels.
  Fit new oil-filter element.
  Lubricate all grease nipples (except steering rack and pinion).
  Lubricate door locks and hinges.
  Clean overdrive filter element.
8. *Wheels and tyres*
  Check tyre pressures.

9,000 miles (15000 km) or 9 months' service

  Carry out the **3,000 miles (5000 km) or 3 months' service.**

12,000 miles (20000 km) or 12 months' service.

1. *Engine*
  Top up carburetter piston dampers.
  Renew air-filter elements.
  Fit new air-pump air cleaners (18GF cars)
  Check valve-rocker clearances, and adjust if necessary.
  Check fan-belt tension.
  Check air-pump belt tension (18GF cars).
  Lubricate water pump sparingly.
  Check coolant level in radiator, and top up if necessary.
  Top up windscreen-washer bottle.
  Crankcase closed breather system; change engine-oil filler cap and clean crankcase breather valve.
  Oscilloscope tune up.
  Check exhaust emission (18GF cars).

2. *Ignition*
   Check automatic retard and advance mechanism.
   Clean, and adjust distributor contact points.
   Lubricate all distributor parts as necessary.
   Fit new sparking plugs.
3. *Clutch*
   Check level of fluid in the hydraulic clutch master cylinder.
4. *Steering*
   Check steering and suspension moving parts for wear.
   Check wheel alignment, and adjust if necessary.
5. *Brakes*
   Check brakes, and adjust if necessary.
   Make visual inspection of brake lines and pipes.
   Check level of fluid in the hydraulic brake master cylinder.
   Inspect disc-brake friction pads and renew if required.
   Inspect and blow out brake linings and drums.
6. *General*
   Tighten rear road spring seat bolts.
7. *Electrical*
   Check battery-cell specific-gravity readings and top up to correct
      level.
   Check headlamp alignment.
   Check all lamps for correct functioning.
8. *Lubrication*
   Change oil in engine.
   Lubricate dynamo bearing.
   Top up gearbox, overdrive (if applicable), and rear-axle oil levels.
   Fit new oil-filter element.
   Lubricate steering rack and pinion.
   Lubricate all grease nipples.
   Clean overdrive filter element.
9. *Wheels and tyres*
   Check tyre pressures.

LUBRICATION CHART

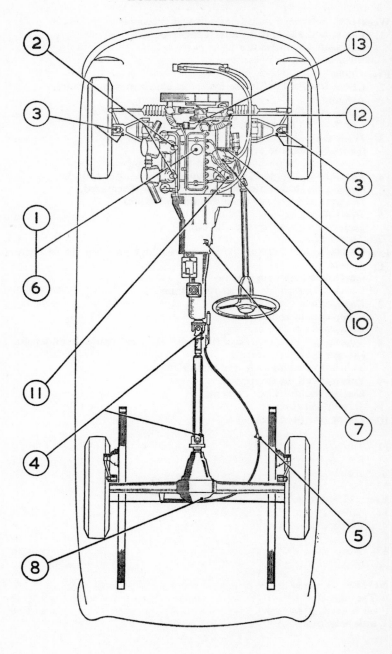

KEY TO LUBRICATION CHART

Weekly
1. *Engine*. Check oil level with the dipstick, and replenish if necessary with new oil to Ref. A.

Every 3,000 miles (5000 km)
2. *Carburetters*. Remove the cap from each suction chamber and insert a small quantity of oil to Ref. E.
Lubricate the carburetter controls.

3. *Front Suspension*. Charge each upper and lower swivel-pin bush and the lower swivel-pin nipple with grease to Ref. C.

4. *Propeller Shaft*. Charge each universal joint nipple and sliding yoke nipple with grease to Ref. C.

5. *Hand Brake Cable*. Charge the nipple on the handbrake cable with grease to Ref. C.

Every 6,000 miles (10000 km)
6. *Engine*. Drain the used oil from the sump and refill to the 'MAX' mark on the dipstick with new oil to Ref. A.

7. *Gearbox and Overdrive*. Check the oil level with the dipstick, and replenish if necessary with new oil to Ref. A.

8. *Rear Axle*. Replenish if necessary to the level of the filler plug with new oil to Ref. B.

9. *Dynamo*. Add two drops of oil to Ref. A to the hole in the rear end bearing plate.

10. *Oil Filter*. Renew the element and wash the bowl in fuel.

11. *Distributor*. Withdraw rotating arm and add a few drops of oil to Ref. A to opening and also to advance mechanism through gap around cam spindle. Smear cam and pivot pin with grease or oil.

Every 12,000 miles (20000 km)
12. *Steering*. (Early cars.) Apply an oilgun containing oil to Ref. B to the nipple and give several strokes.

13. *Water Pump*. Remove the plug on the body and add a small quantity of grease to Ref. C.

NOTES.—Oil and grease references are detailed on page 164.
The engine oil change periods are those recommended when a multigrade oil is used. Monograde or single viscosity oil should be changed at 3,000 mile intervals.

KEY TO RECOMMENDED LUBRICANTS

Component	Engine and Gearbox (A)			Rear Axle and Steering Gear (B)		All Grease Points (C)	Upper Cylinder Lubricant (D)	Oilcan and Carburetter (E)
Climatic conditions predominating	Tropical and temperate down to 5°C (41°F)	Extreme cold temperatures between 5°C (41°F) and −12°C (10°F)	Arctic conditions temperatures consistently below −12°C (10°F)	All conditions down to −12°C (10°F)	Arctic consistently below −12°C (10°F)	All conditions	All conditions	All conditions
BP	Energol SAE 40	Energol SAE 20W Visco-Static	Energol SAE 10W Visco-Static	Gear Oil SAE 90 EP	Gear Oil SAE 80 EP	Energrease L2	Upper Cylinder Lubricant	Visco-Static
CASTROL	Castrol XL	Castrolite	Castrol Z	Castrol Hypoy	Castrol Hypoy Light	Castrolease LM	Castrollo	Castrolite
DUCKHAM'S	Q 20/50	Q 5500	Q 5500	Duckham's Hypoid 90	Duckham's Hypoid 80	Duckham's LB 10 Grease	Duckham's Adcoid Liquid	Q 5500
ESSO	Esso Motor Oil 40/50† Esso Motor Oil 40 Esso Extra Motor Oil 20W/40	Esso Motor Oil 20W/30† Esso Motor Oil 20 Esso Extra Motor Oil	Esso Motor Oil 10W Esso Extra Motor Oil 5W/20	Esso Gear Oil GP 90/140† or GP 90	Esso Gear Oil GP 80	Esso Multipurpose Grease H	Esso Upper Cylinder Lubricant	Esso Extra Motor Oil
FILTRATE	Filtrate Heavy Filtrate 20W/40	Filtrate 10W/30 Filtrate Zero	Filtrate Sub Zero 10W	Filtrate Hypoid Gear 90	Filtrate Hypoid Gear 80	Filtrate Super Lithium Grease	Filtrate Petroyle	Filtrate 10W/30
MOBIL	Mobiloil AF* Mobiloil BB	Mobiloil Special	Mobiloil 10W	Mobilube GX 90	Mobilube GX 80	Mobilgrease MP	Mobil Upperlube	Mobiloil Special
SHELL	Shell Super Motor Oil Shell X—100 40 Shell X—100 Multigrade 20W/40*	Shell Super Motor Oil Shell X—100 10W Shell X—100 Multigrade 10W/30*	Shell Super Motor Oil Shell X—100 10W Multigrade 10W/30*	Shell Spirax 90 EP	Shell Spirax 80 EP	Shell Retinax A	Shell Upper Cylinder Lubricant	Shell Super Motor Oil
STERNOL	WW 40	WW Multigrade 10W/40	WW 10	Ambroleum EP 90	Ambroleum EP 80	Sternoline LHT	Sternol Magikoyl	WW Multigrade 10W/40

* Not available in the United Kingdom.

† Available in the United Kingdom only.

APPENDIX V

WIRING DIAGRAMS

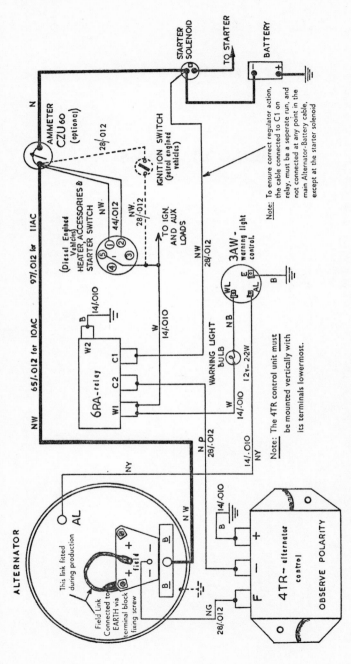

Alternator circuits, showing cable sizes, for positive earth systems on BMC B type engined vehicles
(For cable colour code refer to page 169)

Parts required for Alternator and Ammeter installation on Series III Cars

1	12H 1935	Bracket alternator to crankcase.	
1	12H 1936	Support bracket to crankcase.	
1	12H 2005	Alternator adjusting link.	
1	12A 34	Alternator pulley.	
1	13H 3637	Fan belt (Goodyear)	
1	AHH 8176	Bracket coil mounting (or make from std. bracket).	
2	AHH 6690	Cable clips.	
1	2A 9137	Lucas connector and cover (insulates spare Lucar tag on solenoid).	
1	AHH 7332	Clip.	
1	13H 2131	Alternator	Lucas no. 54021092
1	13H 1864	4 TR control unit	,, ,, 37423
1	13H 1495	6RA relay	,, ,, 33252
1	BMK 1092	3AW warning-light control	,, ,, 38706
1	AHH 8193	Extension wiring harness	,, ,, 54950372
1	BHA 4420	Ammeter	,, ,, 36275
2	BHA 4423	Nipple (clinch on type)	,, ,, 54944095
1	BHA 4424	Nipple (clinch on type)	,, ,, 54941384
1	AHH 8229	Support strap (oil-cooler pipe)	

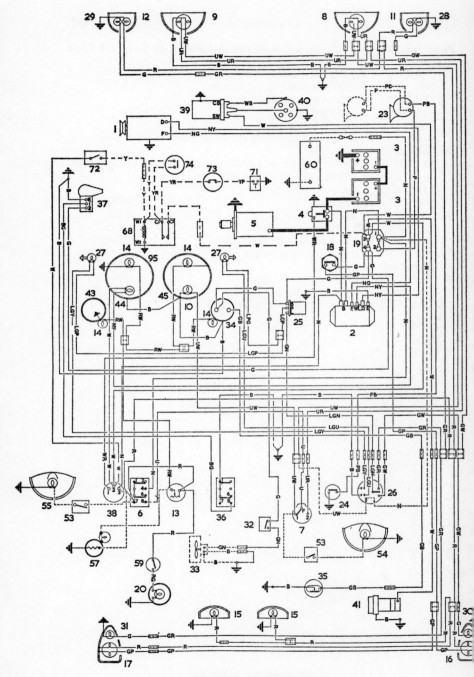

WIRING DIAGRAM

(Early Cars) with positive earth

M

KEY TO THE WIRING DIAGRAM
(Early Cars)

No.	Description	No.	Description	No.	Description
1.	Dynamo	20.	Map light	39.	Ignition coil
2.	Control box	23.	Horn (twin when fitted*)	40.	Distributor
3.	Batteries—6 volt	24.	Horn-push	41.	Fuel pump
4.	Starter solenoid	25.	Flasher unit	43.	Oil-pressure gauge
5.	Starter motor	26.	Direction-indicator (and flasher*) switch	44.	Ignition warning lamp
6.	Lighting switch			45.	Speedometer
7.	Headlamp dip switch	27.	Direction-indicator warning lamps	53.	Fog or driving-lamp switches*
8.	R H headlamp	28.	R H front-flasher lamp	54.	Driving lamp*
9.	L H headlamp	29.	L H front-flasher lamp	55.	Fog lamp*
10.	Main-beam warning lamp	30.	R H rear-flasher lamp	57.	Cigar-lighter—illuminated*
11.	R H sidelamp	31.	L H rear-flasher lamp	59.	Map-light switch
12.	L H sidelamp	32.	Heater or fresh-air motor switch	60.	Radio*
13.	Rheostat—panel lamps	33.	Heater or fresh-air motor*	68.	Overdrive relay unit*
14.	Panel lamps	34.	Fuel gauge	71.	Overdrive solenoid*
15.	Number-plate lamps	35.	Fuel-gauge tank unit	72.	Overdrive manual control switch*
16.	R H stop/tail lamp	36.	Windshield-wiper switch	73.	Overdrive gear switch*
17.	L H stop/tail lamp	37.	Windshield-wiper motor	74.	Overdrive throttle switch*
18.	Stop-lamp switch	38.	Ignition/starter switch	95.	Tachometer
19.	Fuse unit				

Cable Colour Code

N	Brown	P	Purple	W	White
U	Blue	G	Green	Y	Yellow
R	Red	LG	Light Green	B	Black

When a cable has two colour code letters the first denotes the main colour and the second denotes the tracer colour. Items marked thus * may be fitted as optional extras. Their circuits are shown dotted on the Wiring Diagram.

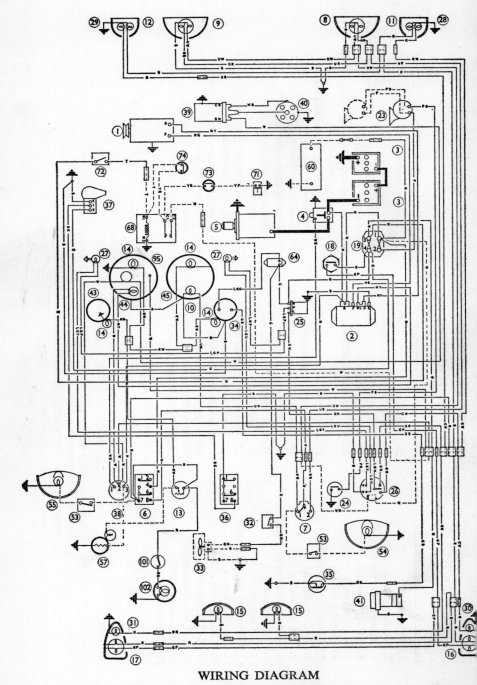

WIRING DIAGRAM

(Later Cars) with positive earth up to but not including GMW4 and GMD4 cars

KEY TO THE WIRING DIAGRAM
(Later Cars)

No.	Description
1.	Dynamo
2.	Control box
3.	Battery—6 volt
4.	Starter solenoid
5.	Starter motor
6.	Lighting switch
7.	Headlamp dip switch
8.	R H headlamp
9.	L H headlamp
10.	Main-beam warning lamp
11.	R H sidelamp
12.	L H sidelamp
13.	Rheostat—panel lamps
14.	Panel lamps
15.	Number-plate illumination lamps
16.	R H stop and tail lamp
17.	L H stop and tail lamp
18.	Stop-lamp switch
19.	Fuse unit
23.	Horn (twin horns when fitted)
24.	Horn-push
25.	Flasher unit

No.	Description
26.	Direction-indicator switch (and flasher switch (when fitted))
27.	Direction-indicator warning lamps
28.	R H front-flasher lamp
29.	L H front-flasher lamp
30.	R H rear-flasher lamp
31.	L H rear-flasher lamp
32.	Heater or fresh-air motor switch
33.	Heater or fresh-air motor (when fitted)
34.	Fuel gauge
35.	Fuel-gauge tank unit
36.	Windshield-wiper switch
37.	Windshield-wiper motor
38.	Ignition/starter switch
39.	Ignition coil
40.	Distributor
41.	Fuel pump
43.	Oil-pressure gauge
44.	Ignition warning lamp
45.	Speedometer

No.	Description
53.	Fog or driving lamp switch (when fitted)
54.	R H fog lamp or R H driving lamp (when fitted)
55.	L H fog lamp or L H driving lamp (when fitted)
57.	Cigar-lighter—illuminated (when fitted)
60.	Radio (when fitted)
63.	Flasher relay (when fitted)
64.	Bi-metal instrument voltage stabilizer
68.	Overdrive relay unit ⎱ when
71.	Overdrive solenoid ⎰ fitted
72.	Overdrive manual control switch
73.	Overdrive gear switch
74.	Overdrive throttle switch (vacuum operated)
95.	Revolution counter
101.	Map light switch
102.	Map light

Cable Colour Code

N	Brown	P	Purple	W	White
U	Blue	G	Green	Y	Yellow
R	Red	LG	Light Green	B	Black

When a cable has two colour letters the first denotes the main colour and the second denotes the tracer colour.

APPENDIX VI

USEFUL PART NUMBERS

Engine unit 18G and 18GA	*Part no.*	*Quantity*
Piston assemblies—grade 3—HC		
Standard	12H 0961 03	4
·010 in. (·254 mm) O/S	12H 0961 13	4
·020 in. (·508 mm) O/S	12H 0961 23	4
·030 in. (·762 mm) O/S	12H 0961 33	4
·040 in. (1·016 mm) O/S	12H 0961 43	4
Piston assemblies—grade 6—HC		
Standard	12H 0961 06	4
·010 in. (·254 mm) O/S	12H 0961 16	4
·020 in. (·508 mm) O/S	12H 0961 26	4
·030 in. (·762 mm) O/S	12H 0961 36	4
·040 in. (1·016 mm) O/S	12H 0961 46	4
Piston assemblies—grade 3—LC		
Standard	12H 0959 03	4
·010 in. (·254 mm) O/S	12H 0959 13	4
·020 in. (·508 mm) O/S	12H 0959 23	4
·030 in. (·762 mm) O/S	12H 0959 33	4
·040 in. (1·016 mm) O/S	12H 0959 43	4
Piston assemblies—grade 6—LC		
Standard	12H 0959 06	4
·010 in. (·254 mm) O/S	12H 0959 16	4
·020 in. (·508 mm) O/S	12H 0959 26	4
·030 in. (·762 mm) O/S	12H 0959 36	4
·040 in. (1·016 mm) O/S	12H 0959 46	4
Rings—compression—top		
Standard	12H 757	4
·010 in. (·254 mm) O/S	12H 0757 10	4
·020 in. (·508 mm) O/S	12H 0757 20	4
·030 in. (·762 mm) O/S	12H 0757 30	4
·040 in. (1·016 mm) O/S	12H 0757 40	4
Rings—compression—2nd and 3rd		
Standard	12H 758	8
·010 in. (·254 mm) O/S	12H 0758 10	8
·020 in. (·508 mm) O/S	12H 0758 20	8
·030 in. (·762 mm) O/S	12H 0758 30	8
·040 in. (1·016 mm) O/S	12H 0758 40	8

Engine unit 18G and 18GA—*cont.*   *Part no.*   *Quantity*

Rings—scraper
Standard   12H 759   4
·010 in. (·254 mm) O/S   12H 0759 10   4
·020 in. (·508 mm) O/S   12H 0759 20   4
·030 in. (·762 mm) O/S   12H 0759 30   4
·040 in. (1·016 mm) O/S   12H 0759 40   4

Reground crankshafts are available (*i.e.* ·010 in. U/S, ·020 in. U/S, ·030 in. U/S) down to ·040 in. undersize. They are supplied complete with bearing shells. The part number is 48G 292 R. To obtain a specific undersized crankshaft it is necessary to make a special request for the size required. Normally (stocks permitting) the request would be fulfilled.

The part number for 1 set standard big-end shells is 8G 2285.

The crankshaft thrust-washers are the same as the 18GB engine.

Engine unit 18GB/18GD/18GF   *Part no.*   *Quantity*

Piston assembly—Grade 3—HC
Standard   8G 2474 03   1 set
·010 in. (·254 mm) O/S   8G 2474 13   1 set
·020 in. (·508 mm) O/S   8G 2474 23   1 set
·030 in. (·762 mm) O/S   8G 2474 33   1 set
·040 in. (1·016 mm) O/S   8G 2474 43   1 set

Piston assembly—Grade 6—HC
Standard   8G 2474 06   1 set
·010 in. (·254 mm) O/S   8G 2474 16   1 set
·020 in. (·508 mm) O/S   8G 2474 26   1 set
·030 in. (·762 mm) O/S   8G 2474 36   1 set
·040 in. (1·016 mm) O/S   8G 2474 46   1 set

Piston assembly—Grade 3—LC
Standard   8G 2475 03   1 set
·010 in. (·254 mm) O/S   8G 2475 13   1 set
·020 in. (·508 mm) O/S   8G 2475 23   1 set
·030 in. (·762 mm) O/S   8G 2475 33   1 set
·040 in. (1·016 mm) O/S   8G 2475 43   1 set

Piston assembly—Grade 6—LC
Standard   8G 2475 06   1 set
·010 in. (·254 mm) O/S   8G 2475 16   1 set
·020 in. (·508 mm) O/S   8G 2475 26   1 set
·030 in. (·762 mm) O/S   8G 2475 36   1 set
·040 in. (1·016 mm) O/S   8G 2475 46   1 set
Circlip-pin   CC 213   8

Engine unit 18GB/18GD/18GF—*cont.*	*Part no.*	*Quantity*
Ring—piston (engine set)		
Standard	8G 2464	1 set
·010 in. (·254 mm) O/S	8G 2464 10	1 set
·020 in. (·508 mm) O/S	8G 2464 20	1 set
·030 in. (·762 mm) O/S	8G 2464 30	1 set
·040 in. (1·016 mm) O/S	8G 2464 40	1 set

Reground crankshafts are available (*i.e.* ·010 in. U/S, ·020 in. U/S, ·030 in. U/S) down to ·040 undersize. They are supplied complete with bearing shells. The part number is 48G 411 R. The previous remarks regarding crankshafts for the 18G/18GA engine apply.

The part number for 1 set standard big-end shells is 8G 2426
,, ,, ,, ,, ,, ,, ,, main bearing shells is 8G 2389.
,, ,, ,, ,, crankshaft thrust-washers (2) std. upper 12B 120.
,, ,, ,, ,, ,, ,, ,, (2) ,, lower 12B 121.
,, ,, ,, ,, ,, ,, ,, (2) ·003 in. O/S upper 12B 0120 03.
,, ,, ,, ,, ,, ,, ,, (2) ·003 in. O/S lower 12B 0121 03.

The latest clutch for the MGB Series III is part number 13H 3935 which should be used with the release bearing 27H 2609.

The difference between each grade of piston is approx. ·0004 in. A grade 4 piston being approx. ·0012 in. larger diameter than a grade 1 piston.

APPENDIX VII

SERVICE TOOLS

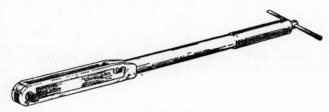

18G536   Torque wrench—2 to 8 lb ft (·28 to 1·11 kg m)
18G537   Torque wrench—5 to 30 lb ft (0·69 to 4·15 kg m)
18G372   Torque wrench—30 to 140 lb ft (4·15 to 19·3 kg m)

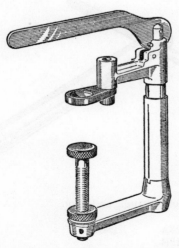

18G45   Valve spring compressor. This tool is lever- and cam-operated, providing easy and quick action.

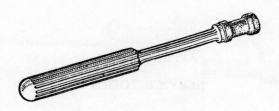

18G29A Suction pad—Valve grinding-in tool. This detachable pad is available to replace a worn rubber pad on tool 18G29.

Tools required for refacing the cylinder head valve seatings

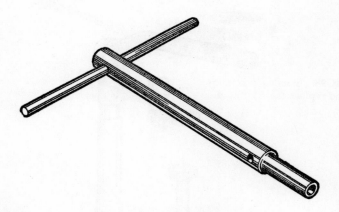

18G27 Valve seat cutter handle and pilot.
Cutters required:

18G25	**18G28A**	**18G28**
18G25A	**18G28B**	
18G174B	**18G28C**	
18G25C	**18G174D**	

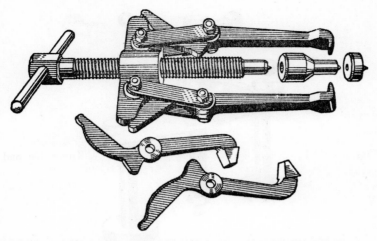

18G2   Crankshaft gear, pulley and propeller shaft flange remover

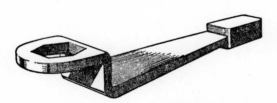

18G98   Starting nut spanner. A shock-type spanner designed to remove and replace the starting dog (when fitted) or the crankshaft pulley bolt.

18G5   First-motion-shaft nut spanner.

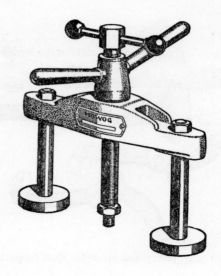

18G42A   Main bearing cap remover (basic tool)

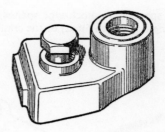

18G42C   Main bearing cap remover adaptor. For use with main bearing
cap remover 18G42A.

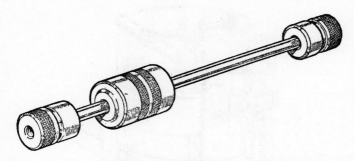

18G284 Impulse extractor—UNF (basic tool). With the adaptor 18G284A this extractor will remove the most difficult main bearing cap quickly, without damage.
Alternatively, 18G42A may be used.

18G284A Main bearing cap remover adaptor—UNF. For use with impulse extractor 18G284. Alternatively, 18G42A may be used.

18G69 Tool for holding the oil release valve, for lapping-in.

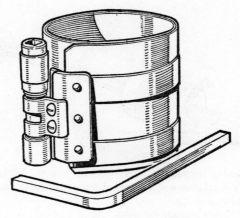

18G55A   Piston ring compressor

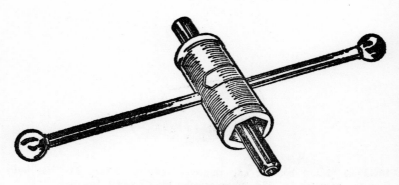

18G152   Rear hub nut spanner

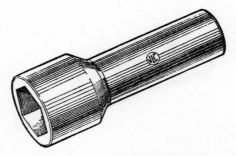

18G586   Rear axle shaft nut spanner (wire wheel)

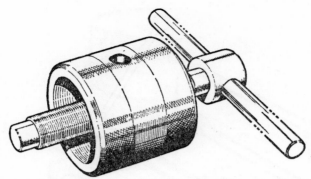

18G363 Wire wheel hub remover (12 t p i). Designed to withdraw left-hand and right-hand hubs. The body is internally threaded with a left-hand thread in one end and a right-hand thread in the other.

18G1032 (8 t p i)

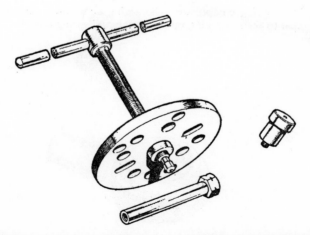

18G304 (Plate and screw), **18G304A** ($\frac{1}{2}$ in. UNF bolt), **18G304B** ($\frac{7}{16}$ UNF bolt) and **18G304J** (rear axle plug) front and rear hub plate remover (basic tool). The plate in combination with two bolts and plug will remove the front and rear hubs with pressed-steel wheels.

18G693 Coil spring compressor. The spring compressor thrust pad is ball-mounted to assist in lining up the spring and spring seat.

18G598 Gearbox front cover centralising tool. Ensures that the front cover oil seal is fitted concentrically with the first motion shaft.

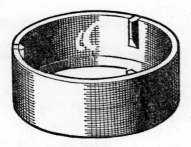

18G222   Synchromesh unit assembly ring—Second speed. Facilitates the assembly of synchroniser and sleeve by enabling the springs and balls to be inserted easily.

18G223   Synchromesh unit assembly ring—Third and top

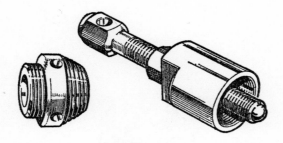

Right : **18G389** Gearbox, rear oil seal remover (basic tool). This basic tool, together with the appropriate adaptor, is essential for removing the gearbox extension oil seal without removing the gearbox from the vehicle. The appropriate adaptor for use with the basic tool is supplied separately.

Left : **18G389B** Gearbox, rear oil seal remover—Adaptor. Used in conjunction with basic tool 18G389, it screws into the end of the oil seal and withdraws it without damage to the rear extension.

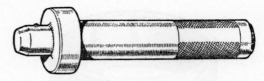

18G134 Bearings and oil seal remover and replacer (basic tool). Used with adaptor 18G134N. Oil seals can be fitted to the gearbox extension without removal from the vehicle.

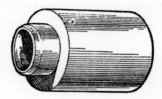

18G134BK Gearbox rear oil seal replacer—Adaptor. For easy replacement of the gearbox extension oil seal. Use in conjunction with 18G134.

APPENDIX VIII

OPTIONAL EXTRAS

	Part No.
Overdrive	See Parts List
Wire wheels	See Parts List
Heater	See Parts List
Fresh-air unit	See Parts List
Fog lamp (Export only—Home through B.M.C. Service Ltd.)	57H 5593
Headlamp flasher	See Parts List
Twin horns, low note (Export only—Home through B.M.C. Service Ltd.)	BCA 4726
Folding de-luxe hood	See Parts List
Tonneau cover	See Parts List
Anti-roll bar	See Parts List
Ashtray (Export only—Home through B.M.C. Service Ltd.)	AHH 5539
Front bumper with overriders (Export only—Home through B.M.C. Service Ltd.)	AHH 6917
Luggage grid (Export only—Home through B.M.C. Service Ltd.)	AHH 6946
Wing mirror (Export only—Home through B.M.C. Service Ltd.)	27H 9863
Radio	See Trade List
Rear compartment cushion (Export only—Home through B.M.C. Service Ltd.)	See Parts List
Cigar-lighter (Export only—Home through B.M.C. Service Ltd.)	AHH 7010
Ace-Mercury wheel discs (Export only—Home through B.M.C. Service Ltd.) R.H.	AHH 7044
L.H.	AHH 7045
Long-range lamp (Export only—Home through B.M.C. Service Ltd.)	57H 5522
Steering-column locks (Germany, Sweden, Austria)	See Parts List
Hardtop	See Parts List

N

APPENDIX IX

COMPETITION EQUIPMENT

General	Part no.	Qty/car
Wire wheel—14 in. with 5½ in. wide rim (60-spoke)	C–AHH 8334	5
Wire wheel—14 in. with 5½ in. wide rim (70-spoke)	C–AHH 8530	5
Bonnet securing straps leather—Tongue half	C–AHH 5519	1
Buckle half	C–AHH 5518	1
Retainer	C–AHH 5517	2
Sebring headlamp cowl kit	C–AJJ 3307	1
Workshop Manual	AKD 3259	1

Brakes

Brake pads (set 4) (Ferodo DS 11)—competition facings	C–8G 8834	1
Rear brake-shoe and lining assembly (set 4) (Ferodo VG 95/1) (competition facings)	C–8G 8828	1
Rear brake lining (with rivets) (set 2) (Ferodo VG 95/1) (competition facings)	C–8G 8829	2
Rear wheel brake cylinder assembly—⅝ in. (15·9 mm) dia.	17H 8773	2
Pawl handbrake lever (for fly-off handbrake)	C–AHH 7223	1
Pawl rod (for fly-off handbrake)	C–AHH 7222	1
Brake servo kit	8G 8732	1

Suspension

Shock absorbers (competition setting)—front	C–AHH 7104	2
Shock absorbers (competition setting)—rear R H	C–AHH 7105	1
Shock absorbers (competition setting)—rear L H	C–AHH 7106	1
Shock absorber valve assembly (only) (competition setting)—front	C–AHH 7217	2
Shock absorber valve assembly (only) (competition setting)—rear	C–AHH 7218	2
Front coil springs ⎤	AHH 6451	2
Front coil springs ⎬ See page 153 for details	AHH 5789	2
Front coil springs ⎦	C–AHT 21	2
Rear road springs ⎤	AHH 7080	2
Rear road springs ⎥	AHH 6453	2
Rear road springs ⎬ See page 153 for details	C–AHH 8343	2
Rear road springs ⎥	AHH 7346	2
Rear road springs ⎦	C–AHT 20	2

Suspension—*cont.*

	Part no.	Qty/car
†Optional extra anti-roll bar—$\frac{9}{16}$ in. (14·3 mm) dia.	AHH 7329	1
Bearing for $\frac{9}{16}$ in. (14·3 mm) anti-roll bar	AHH 6541	2
*Anti-roll bar installation kit	C–AJJ 3306	1
*Alternative $\frac{5}{8}$ in. (15·9 mm) dia. anti-roll bar (with bearings)	C–AHH 7593	1
*Anti-roll bar—$\frac{5}{8}$ in. (15·9 mm) dia.	AHH 7331	1
*Bearing—$\frac{5}{8}$ in. (15·9 mm) dia. anti-roll bar	1B 4526	2
Alternative $\frac{3}{4}$ in. (19 mm) dia. anti-roll bar	C–AHH 7924	1

Contents of kit for fitting anti-roll bar:

	Part no.	Qty/car
Link—anti-roll bar—R H	AHH 6543	1
Link—anti-roll bar—L H	AHH 6544	1
Bearing strap	1B 7356	2
Clamping bolt	AHC 146	2
$\frac{7}{16}$ in. dia. spring washer	LWZ 207	2
$\frac{7}{16}$ in. UNF locknut	BHA 4557	2
$\frac{5}{16}$ in. UNF $\times \frac{5}{8}$ in. hexagon head crew	HZS 0505	4
$\frac{5}{16}$ in. dia. spring washer	LWZ 205	4
$\frac{1}{2}$ in. dia. spring washer	LWZ 208	2
$\frac{1}{2}$ in. UNF hexagon head nut	FNZ 108	2
End location stop	AHH 6546	4
No. 10 recessed pan-head screw	PMZ 0308	4
Spring washer	LWZ 203	4
Nut	FNZ 103	4
Bottom wishbone assembly—R H	AHH 5927	1
Bottom wishbone assembly—L H	AHH 5929	1

Parts required to convert early gearbox to large-diameter layshaft and close-ratio gears:

	Part no.	Qty/car
Gearbox-casing assembly (overdrive)	48G 314	1
Gearbox-casing assembly (non-overdrive)	48G 315	1
Laygear	C–22H 932	1
Layshaft	22H 571 or 22H 465	1
Thrust-washer for laygear (front)	22H 466	1
Thrust-washer for laygear (rear) (or 22H 468, 469, or 470)	22H 467	1
Caged needle-roller bearing (for laygear)	22H 471	4
Distance piece for bearing	22H 672	1
First-motion shaft (18G/18GA only)	C–22H 472	1
First-motion shaft (18GB only)	C–22H 846	1
Second-speed mainshaft gear	C–22H 1094	1
Third-speed mainshaft gear	C–1H 3300	1
Gearbox dipstick (with sealing rings)	AEC 3683	1

* Parts standard fitment on MGB GT.
† Standard fitment Tourer from Chassis no. 108039.

Clutch

Competition clutch-cover assembly	C–BHA 4642	1
Competition clutch-driven plate assembly	C–BHA 4519	1
Graphite thrust-bearing assembly	27H 2609	1
Graphite thrust-bearing retaining spring	22B 66	1

Engine

Crankshaft (induction-hardened heavy duty) (18GB)	C–AEH 822	1
Main-bearing set for hardened crankshaft (18GB)	C–18G 8103	1
Main-bearing set (racing clearances) (18G/18GA)	C–8G 8843	1
Main bearing set (intermediate) (18GB standard crankshaft only)	C–18G 8021	1
Use with main bearing set C–8G 8843		
Packing piece—oil relief valve spring (standard on 18GB)	AEH 798	1
Valve guide—inlet (Hidural)	C–AEH 755	4
Valve guide—exhaust (Hidural)	C–AEH 756	4
Inlet valve—$1\frac{9}{16}$ in. (39·7 mm) dia. (Nimonic)	C–AEH 757	4
Inlet valve $1\frac{11}{16}$ in. (42·8 mm) dia. (Nimonic)	C–AEH 860	4
Exhaust valve—$1\frac{11}{32}$ in. (34·1 mm) dia. (Nimonic)	C–AEH 758	4
Valve spring—inner (57 lb [25·9 kg])	C–1H 1112	8
Valve spring—outer (140 lb [63·5 kg]) ⎫ double	C–AHH 7264	8
Valve spring—inner (60 lb (27·2 kg) ⎭ valve springs	C–AHH 7265	8
Valve spring top cup ⎫ for Nimonic valve	C–AEH 760	8
Valve spring bottom cup ⎭ and double springs	C–AEH 801	8
Valve collets—pairs (for Nimonic valve)	C–AEH 761	8
Valve springs, triple (set of 3)	C–AHH 7309	8
Valve spring cup (for triple springs)	C–AHH 7313	8
Valve rocker—strengthened	12H 2037	8
Rocker shaft bracket—front	C–AEH 762	1
Rocker shaft bracket—rear	C–AEH 763	1
Distance piece for rocker—long	C–AEH 764	1
Distance piece for rockers—short	C–AEH 765	2
Tappet adjusting screw (undrilled)	C–AEH 766	8
Tappet (large diameter)	AEC 264	8
Push-rod	C–AEH 767	8
Cylinder head gasket (competition type)	C–AEH 768	1
Crankshaft chain wheel (steel)	12H 244	1
Camshaft (competition) (Stage 3)	C–AEH 714	1
Camshaft—high-lift—wide-period—full race	C–AEH 770	1
Camshaft chain wheel (steel)	C–AEH 771	1
Connecting rod and cap complete—R H (cylinders 2 and 4) (18G/18GA only)	C–AEH 642	2
Connecting rod and cap complete—L H (cylinders 1 and 3) (18G/18GA only)	C–AEH 644	2
Connecting rod bearing set (18G/18GA only)	8G 2259	1
Connecting rod bearing set (18GB only)	C–18G 8022	1

Engine—*cont.*	*Part no.*	*Qty/* *car*
Piston, with gudgeon pin and rings (18G/18GA only) (Standard or + ·020 in. [·51 mm]). For use with connecting rods C–AEH 642 and C–AEH 644 only	C–AEH 736	4
Piston ring—top	C–AEH 738	4
Piston ring—second and third	C–AEH 854	8
Piston ring—scraper	C–12H 759	4
Gudgeon pin	C–AEH 741	4
Circlip	C–AEH 742	8
Piston, with gudgeon pin and rings (18GB)	C–AEH 853	4
Piston ring—top	C–AEH 738	4
Piston ring—second and third	C–AEH 854	8
Piston ring—scraper	C–12H 759	4

Weber carburetter installation

Carburetter assembly (Weber)	C–AEH 785	1
Weber carburetter installation kit	C–AJJ 3312	1
Contains:		
Inlet manifold complete (for Weber carburetter)	C–AEH 772	1
Stud—carburetter to inlet manifold (long)	C–AEH 775	2
Stud—carburetter to inlet manifold (short)	C–AEH 776	2
Plain washer for stud	PWZ 105	4
Locknut for stud (thin type)	C–AEH 777	4
Stud—steady-rod anchor plate to manifold	CHS 2511	4
Stud—throttle-cable bracket to manifold	CHS 2511	2
Steady rod complete	C–AEH 778	1
Bolt—fork end to bracket or plate	HBZ 0510	2
Nut—fork end to bracket or plate	LNZ 205	2
Washer—fork end to bracket or plate	PWZ 105	2
Anchor plate—inlet manifold—rear	C–AEH 781	1
Nut—anchor plate—inlet-manifold stud	LNZ 205	2
Washer—anchor plate	PWZ 105	2
Anchor nut—steady rod rear plate	C–AEH 843	1
'O' ring—carburetter to manifold	C–AEA 605	2
Nut for carburetter stud	LNZ 205	4
Washer—carburetter stud	PWZ 105	4
Double-coil spring washer	AJD 7732	4
Adaptor union—petrol pipe to carburetter	C–AEH 786	1
Washer for adaptor	6K 638	1
Throttle countershaft—complete	C–AEH 787	1
Bracket—throttle-cable abutment	C–AEH 792	1
Washer for stud—bracket to manifold	PWZ 105	2
Locknut for stud—bracket to manifold	LNZ 205	2
Adaptor—Servo brakes	C–AEH 793	1
Copper washer for adaptor	6K 638	1
Throttle link—lever to carburetter—complete	C–AEH 794	1
Throttle cable	C–AHH 7365	1

		Qty/
Weber carburetter installation—*cont.*	*Part no.*	*car*
Throttle return spring	AHH 5621	1
Manifold gasket (induction)	1G 2417	1
Exhaust-pipe joint	AHH 6358	2
Flexible petrol pipe	AHH 5544	1

Engine ancillaries

Exhaust manifold (lightweight steel, tuned)	C–AHH 7103	1
Pulley—for dynamo (reduced speed)	2A 864	1
Fan belt (for reduced speed pulley)	13H 932	1
Distributor (Competition tune—Lucas no. 40943A)	C–BHA 4415	1
Engine oil sump (deep type) (18G/18GA) 1 in. (25·4 mm)	C–AHH 7252	1
Packing piece for pump strainer (18G/18GA) 1 in. (25·4 mm)	C–AHH 7238	1
Engine oil sump (deep type) (18GB) 1⅜ in. (35 mm)	C–AEH 832	1
Packing piece for pump strainer (18GB) 1⅜ in. (35 mm)	C–AEH 847	1
Carburetters—1¾ in. (44·45 mm) SU pair	C–AUD 229	1
Installation kit—1¾ in. SU carburetters	C–AJJ 3321	1
including flare pipe	C–AHH 7209	2
Blanking sleeve—thermostat by-pass	11G 176	1

Alternative axle ratios

Crown wheel and pinion—Early tourer only		
4·1 : 1 ratio (10/41)	C–ATB 7240	1
4·3 : 1 ratio (10/43)	ATB 7156	1
4·55 : 1 ratio (9/41)	ATB 7146	1
Crown wheel and pinion—'Tubed' axle only		
4·22 : 1 ratio (9/38)	C–BTB 975	1
4·55 : 1 ratio (9/41)	C–BTB 966	1
Limited slip differential—'Tubed' axle only	C–BTB 777	1

Note: Calibrated speedometers for alternative axle ratios are available in km/h or mile/h to special order.

The parts required for fitting a supplementary fuel tank to the trunk

Part no.		*No. off*
A 7174 X	Trunk floor arrangement	Ref
SK 7428 X	Sketch showing modification to trunk floor	Ref
AHH 7094	Tank support—trunk floor	2
PMZ 0306	No. 10 UNF pan-head screws	18
LWZ 303	No. 10 (·190) spring washers	18

Part no.		No. off
FNZ 103	No. 10 UNF nuts	18
AHH 7239	Assembly of 20-gal (24·2 US gal, 90·92 litres) fuel tanks complete. (Drawing)	Ref
AHH 7050	Supplementary tank 10 gal (12·1 US gal, 45·5 litres) capacity	1
AHH 7051	10-gal (12·1 US gal, 45·5 litres) fuel tank (modified standard)	1
AHH 7243	Seal—small—bottom tank to floor	1
AHH 7244	Seal—large—bottom tank to floor	1
AHH 7093	Rubber connecting hose	2
HCS 1622	Connecting hose clips	4
AHH 6253	Tank straps	2
AHH 6257	Rear hanger	2
AHH 6252	Packing strip—tank strap to tank	2
CLZ 0427	Clevis pin	4
PWZ 104	Plain washer	4
ZPS 0205	Split pin	4
HBZ 0418	$\frac{1}{4}$ in. UNF hexagon head bolt	2
PWZ 104	$\frac{1}{4}$ in. plain washer	2
LNZ 104	$\frac{1}{4}$ in. UNF stiffnut	2
SK 7427 Y	Sketch showing hole in trunk lid	Ref
AHH 7241	Filler neck surround	1
HCS 1622	Pipe clip—filler surround to filler neck	1
AHH 7245	Seal—trunk lid to filler neck surround	1
AHH 7240	Quick-release filler cap (B1685D—Enots) (2½ in. [63·5 mm] outside dia. pipe fitting)	1
AHH 7242	Spare wheel—strap and staple assembly	1
PMZ 0306	No. 10 UNF pan-head screws	4
LWZ 303	No. 10 (·190) spring washers	4
FNZ 103	No. 10 UNF nuts	4

Note: 21 and 23 gallon tanks are available (flange type) to special order.

APPENDIX X

PARTS REQUIRED FOR SPECIAL COMPETITION EQUIPMENT

1 Dual petrol pump	
1 Mounting bracket for pump (make up)	
1 Suitable length $\frac{5}{16}$ in. petrol pipe	
1 Interconnecting union	B174OE
4 Petrol pipes (flexible)	AHB 5366
3 Internal tube nuts	AHH 5385
3 Nipples	AHH 5383
3 Unions (pipe end)	2K 5306
2 Single banjo-type connectors	AUC 1833
2 Banjo bolts	AUC 2698
4 Banjo washers	AUC 2141

The pump may be installed so that the centre of the pump is approximately 6 in. from the wheel arch and 21 in. from the rear bulkhead (see plate 13).

The parts required for fitting an additional cold air intake to the car

1 Air intake with flap	14B 7711
1 Gauze	4G 6575
1 Control cable	14B 7782
*(2 or 1) Clip hose to body	AHH 5714
*(4 or 2) Clip hose to intake	HCS 3036
*(3 or 1) Intake flange	14B 7712
*(2 or 1) Hose (air intake)	14B 2749

* Denotes the parts and quantities required when also fitting a cold air intake or carburation purposes.

APPENDIX XI

USEFUL ADDRESSES

Royal Automobile Club,
Motor Sport Division,
31, Belgrave Square,
London SW 1

Sports Car Club of America,
P.O. Box 791,
Westport,
Connecticut

Canadian Automobile Sports Clubs Inc.,
P.O. Box 97,
Willowdale,
Ontario

British Motor Holdings (U.S.A.) Inc.
734, Grand Avenue,
Ridgefield,
New Jersey

British Motor Holdings Canada Ltd.,
P.O. Box 130, Station 'C',
Kenilworth Avenue North,
Hamilton,
Ontario

B.M.C. Special Tuning Department,
MG Car Company,
Abingdon-on-Thames,
Berkshire,
England

The SU Carburetter Company Ltd.,
Wood Lane,
Erdington,
Birmingham 24

Autopower Corporation,   Crash-roll bars
3163 Adams Avenue,
San Diego,
California 92116

Ashley Auto Improvements Ltd., Twyford Road, Bishop Stortford, Herts.	Hardtops
Downton Engineering Works Ltd., Downton, Salisbury, Wilts.	Conversions, etc.
V. W. Derrington Ltd., 159–161 London Road, Kingston-on-Thames, Surrey	Conversions, etc. HRG alloy cylinder heads
Amco Division of America Carry Products Inc., 7425, Fulton Avenue, North Holywood, California 91605.	Accessories
Dynaplastics, Dept. A P.O. Box 3711, 10337, Rush Street, So. El Monte, California	Royal Landau hardtops
Petrol Injection Ltd., Valley Road, Plympton, Plymouth, Devon	Tecalemit-Jackson fuel injection
Jack Brabham (Conversions) Ltd., 131–139, Goldsworth Road, Woking, Surrey	Crankshaft balancing
Auto Transmissions Ltd., Burnsall Road, Coventry	Laycock de Normanville overdrive
Classic Motor Crafts Ltd., 1, Llanvanor Road, London NW2	Bermuda Classic Hardtops
Tudor Webasto Beaconsfield Road, Hayes, Middlesex	Sun-roof conversions

INDEX